"You don't want anger running your life any more than you want your parents running it for you. Easy to read, useful, and honest, Mitch Abblett's book will show you why getting angry is normal, but also that how you use your anger is up to you."

—**Mark Bertin, MD**, author of *Mindful Parenting for ADHD* and *How Children Thrive*

"We all get mad sometimes, and often we beat ourselves up for it afterwards. In his welcome new book, Abblett takes the pathology out of anger. He normalizes it and offers suggestions for ways to transform anger, using it for the benefit of others and also ourselves."

—**Susan Kaiser Greenland**, cofounder of the Inner Kids foundation, and author of *Mindful Games* and *The Mindful Child*

D0089632

the *i*nstant help solutions series

Young people today need mental health resources more than ever. That's why New Harbinger created the **Instant Help Solutions Series** especially for teens. Written by leading psychologists, physicians, and professionals, these evidence-based self-help books offer practical tips and strategies for dealing with a variety of mental health issues and life challenges teens face, such as depression, anxiety, bullying, eating disorders, trauma, and self-esteem problems.

Studies have shown that young people who learn healthy coping skills early on are better able to navigate problems later in life. Engaging and easy-to-use, these books provide teens with the tools they need to thrive—at home, at school, and on into adulthood.

This series is part of the **New Harbinger Instant Help Books** imprint, founded by renowned child psychologist Lawrence Shapiro. For a complete list of books in this series, visit newharbinger.com.

from anger to action

powerful mindfulness tools to help teens harness anger for positive change

MITCH R. ABBLETT, PhD

Instant Help Books
An Imprint of New Harbinger Publications, Inc.

Publisher's Note

This publication is designed to provide accurate and authoritative information in regard to the subject matter covered. It is sold with the understanding that the publisher is not engaged in rendering psychological, financial, legal, or other professional services. If expert assistance or counseling is needed, the services of a competent professional should be sought.

In consideration of evolving American English usage standards, and reflecting a commitment to equity for all genders, "they/them" is used in this book to denote singular persons.

Book printed in the United States of America

Distributed in Canada by Raincoast Books

Copyright © 2019 by Mitch R. Abblett
New Harbinger Publications, Inc.
5674 Shattuck Avenue
Oakland, CA 94609
www.newharbinger.com

Cover design by Amy Shoup

Acquired by Jess O'Brien

Edited by Karen Schader

All Rights Reserved

Library of Congress Cataloging-in-Publication Data on file

Printed in the United States of America

21   20   19

10   9   8   7   6   5   4   3   2   1   First Printing

Contents

Foreword   vii

Introduction: The Incredible Hero Inside the Angry Hulk   1

Part 1: Listen to Anger

1 Checking Yourself Before You Wreck Yourself   13

2 Translating the Language of Anger   33

3 Feeling It to Heal It   53

Part 2: Look for Your Power

4 The Truth Inside Anger   81

5 Using Anger as Fuel   109

Part 3: Leap Toward Change

6 Action Is Power   127

Conclusion: Break the Dam—Let Your River Flow   145

Acknowledgments   149

Resources   151

Foreword

When Mitch told me he was writing yet another book about teens and anger, I thought, *Really? I know he's worked as a therapist with teens for many years, but he's one of the least angry-looking guys I know.*

And yet, as you'll learn in these pages, anger is not the same for everyone: neither in terms of how it feels nor in how we act. Many people, including both of our teen selves, have a less-than-healthy relationship with anger—not because we lash out at everyone in sight, but because we bottle up and bury our anger inside. However, according to Mitch, it's not about whether you act out your anger, or whether you shove it down inside yourself that really matters. Rather, it's whether you're willing to use skills like mindfulness to actually pay attention to how your anger ends up holding you back from the things that you value, and how it separates you from the people you want in your life.

As a fellow psychologist, mindfulness nerd, and therapist who has sat with hundreds, maybe thousands of teens over the years, I think Mitch is onto something important. Don't read this book because your parents are making you. Don't read it because someone is bribing you, or because your therapist handed it to you. Don't read it expecting to "solve" your anger problems and make them "go away." *Read this book for yourself to get what you want out of life.* Mitch has some good stuff to teach about using your attention to listen to your body, to your thoughts, and to the world around you. This clear listening will, in turn, help you see the important things that your anger may have been hiding from you, and it will help you turn your unhealthy anger into the fuel you'll need to change not only your life, but also the world around you.

I've listened to my own anger more mindfully over the years since I was an angry teen. I've looked more clearly at my life and at my relationships with friends, colleagues, and family, and I've harnessed so much power to go so much further in life than where my misguided, unharnessed anger ever could've taken me—certainly further than my family, friends, or therapist thought I might achieve when I was younger. This book speaks with honesty and authenticity, and it's totally bullshit-free. These are qualities that I appreciate about Mitch as a therapist, a friend, and as a writer. But I trust you'll be the judge of that for yourself.

Bottom line: Read Mitch's book because I told you to!

—Christopher Willard, PsyD,
 Part-time faculty at Harvard Medical School
 Full-time former angry-kid

introduction

The Incredible Hero Inside the Angry Hulk

Have you ever been told to calm down and found yourself wanting to unleash havoc on the person—show them what anger really looks like? Give them a taste of your fire and fury?

If so, you've come to the right place. As you read, ask yourself:

- Do you find yourself regularly hating on certain people? Why do they tick you off?

- Are others keeping you from getting what you want?

- Do adults get you? Do they understand what your life is like?

- Do you ever feel like things are out of control?

- Do you hate it when adults assume things about you—what you can and can't do, perhaps, or what your "problems" are?

I'm guessing the answers to these questions might shine a light on why you feel angry from time to time.

In this book, I'll help you learn how to manage your anger in an empowering way. I promise not to lecture you. I bet you get enough of that already, and I bet it doesn't really help.

Instead of telling you what you should do with your life, I hope to show you how to relate to your daily experiences in a flexible, easy way. I'll encourage you to get real with yourself as to how you think and feel. I'll support you in making decisions that serve you (and others) better.

So, if you're looking for advice about how to solve your problems, this book probably isn't what you're looking for. If you're interested in learning how to manage your feelings (particularly the angry ones) from the inside out—using mindfulness skills that will make your life easier, now and later—then you're in the right place.

Anger Is a Message

Anger shows up to serve a purpose: to send you a message that something's up. Something's not right, and it may need to be dealt with. Anger is not random, and it's not a sign that you're crazy. It's valid—and important.

No one blames an animal in the wild when it strikes out in order to maintain its survival. Why should it then be wrong that you—also a living, breathing animal—push back at the world when it threatens you? And I'm sure there've been many times when you've witnessed adults (even the put-together ones) getting ticked off—so why should you be any different?

Anger is telling you what's important to you, by showing you how you feel when what's important to you is threatened, disregarded, or blocked in some way. When you get super angry at a friend, a teacher, or a family member, you're not doing so randomly—you're not just looking for a little late-afternoon shot of energy. You're getting activated because something real inside you feels like it's not being seen, or like it's being wronged. Your work is to learn to understand this message and to express it in a healthy way—to learn to speak "your truth."

Anger may build up when you feel like you're not getting enough RSVP:

Respect—When adults or even peers don't treat you with the respect you deserve: really listening to what you say, trusting you, believing in you. I'm betting you are more capable than many adults will ever admit.

Space—We all need the physical and emotional room to try things out: to explore life without constant rules, reminders, and responsibility. To be our own person and learn who that is. And sometimes you just want to be alone—to be in a place that feels like it's yours and yours alone.

Validation—You probably experience things pretty intensely. Most teens' emotions are strong and ever changing. Do you ever wish that other people understood this— and that they would know you're not insane?

Provisions (and time with **p**eers). Unless you're already pulling a six-figure salary, you're reliant on the sustenance, shelter, and other support that adults provide. Financial resources are also often needed for you to connect with your peers. Maybe clothes and screens seem essential to acceptance, or maybe you just want to see a movie on Friday with your bestie. When resources are limited, resentment and anger can build.

So what does all this have to do with you? I'm guessing you have no grand plan to screw with people. You don't wake up in the morning, give your villain's mustache a devious twist, and think, *I'm going to unload on as many people as I can today!*

In all seriousness, I'm guessing that actually, when you open your eyes first thing in the morning, some part of you hopes that …

… someone will notice you

… someone will accept you

… you'll get some respect

… you'll have some fun

… you'll excel at something

… and someone will notice.

Mindfulness: Your New Superpower

This book is about taking the normal, healthy experience of anger, and learning to look at it more skillfully and use it in ways that serve you and others. Anger is present in all our lives— you are not alone in feeling it. This book is about using mindful awareness of what's happening in the present moment, without judging it.

Mindfulness isn't religious or mystical, nor is it about getting rid of all thoughts or completely Zen-ing out so that you don't care about anything anymore. You've already, in the course of your life, been mindful *many* times—you just may not have had a word for it. You weren't mindful of your mindfulness.

Perhaps you were

- playing a sport and completely engrossed in action or strategy, or both;

- hanging out with friends, with nothing else in the world seeming relevant or important; or

- working on a project or assignment that completely absorbed your attention.

Mindfulness combines three factors: intention, attention, and attitude. Later in the book I'll rework these factors into the acronym AMP, to hopefully make it easier to remember when you really need it.

A time machine is a device that can take you to some point in either the past or future, right? Think of mindfulness as a time-*less* machine—technology that takes you firmly and deeply into the present moment, making it richer and more meaningful and making you way more effective—and much less ruled by anger.

Here's another way to think about it: Mindfulness is the moments of your daily life that you've truly "owned." Moments when you were completely in tune with/aware of your senses and your thoughts, when you were paying attention to your present experience, on purpose, and without judging it—just noticing.

But you don't have to just wait for these states to pop up. With mindfulness, you actually practice making them happen. You do this by building up the mental "muscle" of mindful attention: noticing what's there, being aware of what's in your senses and thoughts while also letting them play out without trying to control them. When you're in the moment, you own the moment—not by forcing it to be a certain way, but by opening yourself up to every nugget of opportunity.

Mindfulness is a purposeful activity of the mind: focusing on and opening up to what's happening in and around you. With a well-toned mindfulness muscle, you stack the deck in favor of meeting any daily school, peer, and family challenges that come at you. Reactive, lashing-out (or burrowing-in) anger may begin to fade as an "old" strategy once you learn to harness anger's power with mindfulness.

How to Use This Book

I'm going to give you tools that have helped me and many other kids and adults transform anger into something useful and powerful. We're not talking about beating your anger into submission or shoving it into some mental or emotional closet—just the opposite. Anger, when handled with care and attention, can actually become a superpower of sorts. It can be a source of fuel for energized, productive action.

You will learn to recognize all the components of anger:

- its *pain* (how it stirs up your body and mind)

- its *wisdom* (how it shows you and others what's most important to you, what feels most real and alive)

- its *power* (how it gives you emotional fuel for dealing with hard stuff and taking actions that will help you rather than hurt you)

This book is designed to give you a new and lasting way to change how you relate to anger. I recommend bite-size reading, just enough to pick up something new—a new understanding, or maybe a new way to practice being aware of things in the moment. You might try to apply a certain technique to an ongoing situation in your life, for example. Keep it real and keep it manageable. If you scan a section and don't feel it applies to you, skip it. You have enough homework to do. This book is meant to make your life easier; only you know how to put its principles into practice, and to make this stuff part of you in a meaningful and lasting way.

Throughout the book, you'll find three key features within each chapter:

- *Real Talk* is real teens (some of whom are former therapy clients of mine or students with whom I worked, with all their personal details changed to protect their privacy) telling you, in their own words, how they learned to rework their perspective (what I call giving themselves a "mind-set reset") and how it helped them manage their anger. They're not perfect, but they offer us lots to learn from.

- *Give It a Go* sections offer short and not-too-painful practice exercises so you can try out your new skills on your own or with others. Some of the practices emphasize awareness, concentrations, or attention to the present moment. Others focus on insight, and still others on compassion and self-compassion. These are all useful tools for your various life challenges, and they can help you manage anger like a pro.

- *Profile in Power* presents engaging and entertaining (hopefully) anecdotes and quotes from celebrities, athletes, and others. Here, you'll read stories of how teens (both famous and ordinary) harnessed the raw fuel of their anger in healthy, productive, and powerful ways. They may have suffered from the ill effects of their anger, but they also learned how to tame it along the way.

At the end of each chapter, I'll ask you to pause and take a "nav check"—a check-in to make sure you're heading in the right direction. These sections will summarize the key themes of a chapter and point you toward what you can expect in the chapter to follow. So, as we finish this introduction, let's check our internal GPS.

We've talked about how anger is a natural response, and we've looked at how anger is a message for you about things that need to be addressed. Does this resonate for you? Understanding that anger is actually universal, are you able to start cutting yourself some slack?

I've given you a basic overview of what mindfulness is and how it might help you shift your anger—from something that smashes things into something you can use on your way to your best self. If you've ever tried to practice mindfulness, how did it help you—or not? If you haven't tried it, are you curious as to how you might benefit?

In chapter 1, we dive in with a look at how we can start to get a better handle on anger by "listening" more closely to it—building the skills to pick up on the messages that it's sending about what's not working in your life.

Part 1

Listen to Anger

chapter 1

Checking Yourself Before You Wreck Yourself

The summer after eighth grade, I was fourteen and desperately in love with a girl named Sarah—who, of course, had no idea. One day, I stared up into the clouds in my backyard, sweat dripping down my face as I daydreamed, completely forgetting the gas-powered weed trimmer in my hands.

I was going to start the school year with a declaration of my love. I ran through various scenarios in my mind—perhaps I'd move up alongside her in the hallway and make my feelings known. I could see it so clearly. She'd smile and throw her arms around me. Onlookers would burst out in applause. "I can't believe it!" Sarah would breathe into my ear as we held each other. "I've always wanted to be with you."

"What the hell are you doing!" a voice interrupted. It was my older brother, Todd, standing behind me.

Cue much yelling, swearing, bumping of chests, threats of early death … until our mother stepped in and banished us to our respective rooms, but not before my brother yanked the trimmer from my hands and threw it to the ground. "Leave it!"

he yelled. "I guess I'll come back later and actually do your own damn chore so you have more time to daydream like an idiot."

Was I angry? Of course. Could this have gone another way? Certainly. Anger isn't bad—but how we *relate* to it may be less than skillful. Which can lead to negative results in school, sports, relationships, and ... well ... everything.

Is your anger getting in your way? Before doing anything else, it's important to get your bearings and listen to what anger is trying to tell you. It's not just that you should look before you leap—I suggest you listen, then look, then leap.

Listen, Look, Leap

If you're like most teens I've talked to, you may be finding that trying to control your anger isn't working out very well. Perhaps you're ready for a new method? I call this one the Three Ls:

Listen to anger's pain. Mindfulness helps you hear what your body and mind are telling you about your inner experience of the world, which helps get you ready to ...

Look for the wisdom of its message. When you're mindful, you can see the world with clear, undistorted vision. Then, you can see what's required to effectively manage what's in front of your face. Then (and only then) can you ...

Leap from a place of power toward healthy things that matter to you. You can take a well-timed action to respond and deal with what life has brought you today.

Let's look at this process in slow motion. I'll provide an example for us to break down.

Example: Your parent has just asked you a question and, for the millionth time, immediately changed the subject, indicating that they (a) didn't hear you and (b) don't actually care.

- **Listen**

  What does your inner sense of your body and your mind say about this? Perhaps you are hurt or angry that this parent seems to care more about him- or herself than about you. Maybe you're tired of this happening all the time and wish they would just stop asking. Feeling this pain is hard, but it will give you the answers you need to move through it and on to the next step.

- **Look**

  What wisdom can be found here? We look with clarity after we've listened fully, and in so doing, we can see the best move to make. Maybe you can think about talking to this parent about their behavior, if that feels safe—especially if this situation is something that happens a lot. You don't even necessarily need to say anything except to voice your feelings on the subject. They probably have no idea how they're affecting you, and how they're undermining your relationship with them. If you don't feel safe taking this action, you could think of a caring friend or family member you could talk to about the situation—either asking for other positive suggestions you might not have thought of, or just getting support. What action would be meaningful to you and others involved?

- **Leap**

  Maybe you decide to not say anything now, but instead to respond to your parent in the moment the next time this happens (which you know all too well it will). You will be prepared, after thinking this through, and can act with effectiveness instead of reacting with rage and then wasting energy wallowing in regret. Leaping is about taking the risk in order to expand your life, make your mark, or connect with what matters.

To help this process really sink in, try to remember a tough moment that led to much lashing out and flailing about. Now try to imagine using the Three Ls to help guide you through it to a better outcome. Try **listening** to what was happening in and around you, **looking** deeply at what anger had to teach you, and imagine **leaping** toward actions that give your anger a healthy outlet. This is what harnessing your anger and finding your personal power are all about! You'll be hearing a lot more about the Three Ls in this book. If you learn to use them skillfully, your life may surprise you, opening up in ways you never could have imagined!

The Dark Side of Anger

Anger makes it hard to think. It restricts your ability to think clearly, creating a sort of tunnel vision that makes it more likely you'll miss the finer points of the situation you're in. The science is clear that anger makes us more likely to distort our view of others and the world around us. You probably don't even need convincing about this. Just check in with your own past experience. That's likely all the data you'll need to be convinced that anger makes you much less likely to see others (and situations) with the clarity required to solve problems, and really get your needs met.

Anger makes you selfish. It narrows your attention to the threat of the moment—whatever (or whoever) is threatening what's important to you. Think of it from a biological point of view. If a lion never experienced "anger," it wouldn't last very long in the wild. It wouldn't eat! It also wouldn't be able to defend itself or its young. You too experience anger in order to fight off threats *and* to go after things that seem vital to you.

Focusing on the threat angle of anger, evolution built our bodies and minds to react with a fight-or-flight pattern of behavior in order to ward off dangers. And even though we don't usually face daily physical threats to life and limb, our brains don't know the difference—we still have pretty much the same brains of our prehistoric, saber-tooth-tiger–dodging ancestors. While they used anger to fight off tigers and marauding rivals, we use it to fend off (and fire off) nasty text messages and tweets. Our biology doesn't care how "advanced" the threat is.

Whether the threat is physical, social, or psychological, we are wired to react with anger. Let this understanding seep thoroughly into your system. Then, hopefully, you can cut yourself some slack next time you find yourself boiling mad. (And remember: unfortunately, our legal system, teachers, college admissions committees, and potential romantic partners tend to be less forgiving than we'd like.)

Anger can harden you if not skillfully managed. It sets our minds toward a "me versus them" mentality. It separates you from others in your life. Instead of seeing clearly how interconnected you are with others and the world around you, anger deposits you on a desert island all by yourself ... and puts a cannon on the beach with you, so you can fire out at others, on their islands.

It's this solid, unwieldy tendency of the angry mind that, while it might have helped you survive tens of thousands of years ago, does you no favors with your chem teacher who seems to have it in for you. The angry mind needs careful, compassionate bridge building—not bridge burning, which tears down the connections you've built up and can limit your options for the future.

Darth Vader said, "Give yourself to the Dark Side." I say, see the darkness that's there, and shine your light on it.

Be the Change You Wish to See

"I don't need a damn map," I said to myself as I passed the ranger's station. I had been a Boy Scout patrol leader and believed I could rely on my intuitive and impressive sense of direction to guide me through the woods.

I spent a long time in those woods. When it was nearly dark, I panicked and got completely turned around on the trails. Though I was putting in a ton of effort, moving rapidly through the woods, the tunnel vision and stuckness inside me grew as the sun dimmed. Sheer effort was simply not going to get me out of there. I was either going to sleep (and, in my mind, die) there, or I was going to come up with a new plan. A new mind-set. My old way of doing things was not working.

First, I calmed myself down. My mind had been running wild with panicked thoughts of getting eaten in the dead of night in the woods, but I slowed down, caught up with my rapid breathing, and settled in for a minute or two of deep, mindful breaths. I needed to reset my body and my mind. Then I set about walking in a straight line to a tree in the distance. Once there, I drew an imaginary straight line to another tree in the same direction, and I continued in this way until I intersected with a road. Three miles later, I made it to my car, now alone in the dark parking lot.

Only with intention, or willingness to make a change, does effort lead to effective change. Notice I said willingness, not wantingness. It's not about simply saying "Please yes!" to change— it's about being willing to do the work. Willingness is moving forward even when things feel sticky and unpleasant, even when it's really not fun. If we wait until we feel like moving, we might never get anywhere.

Is your usual way of dealing with your thoughts, feelings, and actions regarding anger working for you? Is it giving more than it takes? If it is, great! If not—that's also great. That's why we're here.

If your old ways are not working, are you willing to consider alternatives? Are you willing to find a new path through the woods?

The following questions may help you navigate so you don't get lost like I did:

- How has anger helped you? What does it do for you?

- What does your anger look and feel like?

- How does it get in the way? Does it cost you anything? Hurt you in any way?

AMP Yourself Up

Remember our working definition of mindfulness from the introduction—that whether we're talking about school, sports, time with your friends, or even at home with your family, to be mindful is to combine intention, attention, and attitude.

Here's another way of saying it. You AMP yourself up when you're

Aware on purpose of the

Moment at hand as it

Plays itself out (and without judging).

To understand what's happening inside you with intense anger, you need to tune into what's happening moment to moment, rather than turning away from it. This can be scary, I know, but it gives you valuable intel. To work effectively with anger, you need to pay attention to what it's telling you, and *how* it's telling you. This is where AMPing up and being mindful can be really helpful—and not just for teens but for all of us. I AMP up all the time!

Being in the present is really an opportunity to let go of the past, whether it's upsetting things that have happened, or just something less than perfect you said at a party. It also means letting go of worrying about the future, whether it's who you'll go with to prom, how you'll do on your SATs, or what kind of mess this country will be in by the time you're an adult.

In the present moment, you can just hang out with what's true—what's actually happening. The present moment also doesn't last very long, and it's the only time when you actually have the power to do anything. Surprising research in mindfulness and positive psychology tells us that what we're doing matters less to our happiness than how much we're paying attention to what we're doing.

Here's our first Profile in Power—a true story about a teen whose anger caused a lot of pain and destructiveness, but with work and support, was channeled into personal power.

Profile in Power: Training to Excel

A former therapy client (I'll call him Grant) was fourteen when I first met with him. After a childhood of neglect and abuse from his parents, Grant had trouble dealing with his pent-up rage. He yelled, swore, and, at times, hit people; he even bit his middle school principal, sending her to the hospital.

The adults who cared about him kept looking past his angry actions to the good kid behind the anger, and he slowly (very slowly) began trusting that at least some of these people occasionally meant what they said about him—that he was not merely trash to be thrown away, but instead that he had a wealth of potential inside him.

From a very young age, Grant had a love of trains. He loved reading about them online and riding them. He memorized the types of trains and their schedules. Trains were reliable where his own family had not been. He was drawn to this predictability, as well as to their raw power.

Over time, Grant learned to second-guess his angry, mistrustful thinking and to believe that what others saw in him might actually be his reality. He started reaching out and trusting others, and he got himself an internship with his city's transit authority. After high school, Grant landed a job that had him in and around trains every day.

He's now in his mid-twenties and is an engineer, driving thousands of hardworking folks like himself to and from work each day. His anger, which once fueled his rage, now becomes a kind of fuel for the massive trains he drives. From anger to action, for sure.

Give It a Go: Mindfulness Road Trip

We all grip our thoughts and feelings too tightly from time to time. Particularly when we're upset, we can end up tight and tense. But as one variation of an oft-repeated saying goes, "It's not about the destination, it's about the journey." Mindfulness can be like a road trip with your friends, if you can let go a little. If you're willing, try the following:

1. Set a timer on your phone for between three and five minutes.

2. Sit in an upright, open posture. Don't slouch, but don't be too rigid either. Just sit up so that you're alert. Lay your hands gently on your thighs, palms

up. Take a few slow, deep breaths, bringing the air down into your belly.

3. When you're ready, close your eyes and focus your attention on the sensations of either your left or right hand.

4. As you inhale your next breath, ball your hand into a fist and hold it as tightly as you can for several seconds. As you exhale, release and open your hand, palm facing up. Repeat this process, focusing your attention on slowly and deeply inhaling and exhaling, matching your hand movements as you go.

5. Keep your attention on your breath and on the opening and closing of your fist. If you get distracted (by sounds, other bodily sensations, thoughts, or images), no worries! Don't beat up on yourself. Just come back to the inhaling and exhaling, the closing and opening of your hand, until the timer sounds.

That is mindfulness. It's simple, but not easy. The most important thing is that you are gentle on yourself as you go.

AMP up your attention to what's happening in and around you: be aware of the moment now as it plays out without judgments and overthinking.

Following are some more samples of mindfulness practice. We'll be building on these in the chapters to come. You don't have to sit on a cushion or move to a mountaintop to practice mindfulness. Just bring present-moment awareness to anything you do—eating, bathing, chores, walking, art, performing, practicing, studying. Actually, noticing what's happening, rather than spinning out into the past or future, leads directly to happiness.

Give It a Go: Say Cheese

This brief practice will make your dentist smile. You have to brush your teeth anyway, so you might as well AMP it up while you do.

The next time you go to brush your teeth, instead of rushing through it like most of us do, try this:

1. Pause, with toothbrush in hand, and be fully aware of what you're about to do.

2. Let yourself feel every sense (the sight of the brush, the sound of the water, the smell and taste of the toothpaste, the feel of the brush on your teeth) from moment to moment as you slowly brush your teeth.

3. Let the brushing play itself out without rushing. If your thoughts start pulling at you to finish up and get out of there, try hanging out with the gentle awareness of what you're doing for just a few seconds longer.

Does it feel different to brush this way? Did it leave you feeling cleaner, perhaps, and maybe even more relaxed?

Now let's pause for a quick bite. (I know, I know—you just brushed your teeth!) This exercise illustrates what mindfulness looks and feels like, and it can begin leading you toward a healthier relationship with food in your daily life.

Give It a Go: Meditation on Chocolate Cake

Ready for a thick slice of my chocolate-cake meditation? If you're not a chocolate lover, substitute whatever your sweet tooth fancies.

1. With eyes closed, and sitting up alert yet relaxed, take a deep breath into your belly, exhale, and repeat. Set a timer for sixty seconds.

2. Your only task for this minute is to continue breathing and do whatever you can to force thoughts or images of chocolate cake from your mind. Don't allow cake to touch your imaginary lips for one second!

3. After the timer sounds, keep your eyes closed and notice the overall feel of things internally. What's happening in your mind and body?

4. Gently rest your awareness on your breath. If your mind wanders in any way (to another sensation, image, or thought—even chocolate cake), simply and gently return your attention to the feeling of breathing.

5. Once again, set your timer for sixty seconds and, during this minute, continue anchoring your attention to your breathing, gently returning from any thoughts or mental images, even of cake.

6. Again, after the timer sounds, take an internal weather report, and consider the following questions:

- Which of these two ways of managing thoughts and images of cake required more effort?

- Which led to more thoughts of cake?

- What manages your relationship to cake craving better: force or control (the first method) or mindfulness (the second method)?

Of the hundreds of people I've done this exercise with over the years, the vast majority find a mindful approach (the second method) more effective in managing or relating to the internal experience of chocoliciousness. Control and force leave people feeling exhausted.

And yet, when it comes to dealing with angry thoughts and feelings in your body, which method do you usually use?

This habit of ours to forcefully control our thoughts and feelings turns us into judge, jury, and executioner—of ourselves and others around us. It's not just teens, and it's not just people who struggle with anger—we all do it.

Ask yourself, *How many times has beating myself up in my thoughts actually produced desirable results?* You can't hate yourself into losing weight, or doing better in school, or winning a game.

How often has "I suck" led to awesomeness? Or any of the other harsh stories we tell about ourselves and others:

"I'm not good enough."

"People are always screwing with me."

"I should just give up."

"Others are letting me down."

"This is completely unfair."

"I don't care what people think."

"I'm unlovable."

"I'll never succeed, so why should I even try?"

Mindfulness practices can be very helpful in learning to simply sidestep the inner tongue-lashings we give ourselves and others. Simply step to the side, and let the thought pass you by. If you do, it loses its power over you.

Case Dismissed: Silence Your Inner Judge

Most people, including successful adults, struggle with judgmental thoughts. This contest is where not identifying with the thoughts can be so helpful. It means you don't have to believe everything you think, and it helps you realize that feelings aren't facts.

If you've been living your whole life thinking otherwise, this may sound strange at first. I'm not saying that your thoughts are wrong or that your anger (or other emotions) isn't valid. What I am saying is that negative thinking doesn't help move things forward—it keeps things stuck. You are welcome to hang on to your thoughts or feelings—no one but you has any say over them. But keep in mind, the way they play out is not the only show in town.

Things change. This is one of the only things we can count on to always be true. It can be a relief to remember this when we're in the middle of something hard.

And when we watch our inner experience of ourselves, others, and the world with mindfulness, we see firsthand that thoughts, feelings, and sensations all come and go. For many of us, it's when we can't let our thoughts and feelings play out in the present moment—when we fight against them or pass judgment on them—that we find ourselves really stuck. Because we have to feel them in order for them to pass through us—resisting them only slows down the process.

Mindfulness is essential to this work. It throws you a life vest when you start drowning in rigid, angry thoughts and feelings. By learning to AMP up and bounce your attention back to what is actually happening, you build the muscle of concentration. You train your mind to stay in the present moment.

And by noticing and labeling where your mind goes, you start to get to know your mind better, to learn its triggers, patterns, and habits. This information is crucial because it makes the whole process much more efficient, acting as a form of shorthand—making all of this just a little bit easier next time you do it.

And by being gentle and kind with yourself, you're also creating a new habit of being compassionate toward yourself—something most of us are not in the habit of doing, especially when we're really and truly enraged.

Real Talk: Paul in a Pickle

Here's our first Real Talk, from a seventeen-year-old boy named Paul. His angry outbursts had piled up over the years, leading to two psychiatric hospitalizations; a probation officer (following a fight in the parking lot at school); constant conflict and raw resentment with his dad; and almost costing him his spot on the varsity football team.

"People were always flipping out at me because of my anger. For a long time, I didn't even care. To me, they couldn't handle me being so real and in their faces. I literally believed that. I was pumping with anger all the time and didn't know why, and I felt like some sort of bomb that was wired wrong—always about to go off if you handled it too roughly. But for a long time, I just thought that was who I was. I didn't see any way other than flashing red and letting people have it if they ticked me off."

Paul's view of himself (and his experience of anger) was as solid and unmovable as a giant boulder, and until he learned a new approach, he ran the risk of messing up big time.

Mind-set Reset

As we'll talk about more in the next chapter, our mind-set either helps us see how stressful things, people, and situations can be improved, or it weighs us down with its solid, rigid mass, blocking us and causing some serious daily life damage. Our mind-set is our way of looking at ourselves and the world. In every chapter, we'll show a teen doing the work of shifting toward more fluid, flexible, and mindfully effective thinking.

Paul said he didn't care about the effects of his anger—that he was just being "real" by lashing out at others, and that that was just who he was. Imagine him thinking these sorts of thoughts, and feeling the anger pumping through his body when he saw his friend from the football team standing close to his former girlfriend (who had dumped him because of his angry outbursts). It looked to Paul like this jackass was hitting on *his* girlfriend. He could feel his pulse surging. To him it was go time, and he had a right to let his soon-to-be-former-friend have it.

Can you see how tunnel vision was affecting Paul? How he's actually separating from what's happening versus getting clear about it?

By listening closely to what his thinking (mind) and feeling (body) selves are saying, Paul figured out what was sparking his anger in the first place. As we talked about in the intro, there's a message to anger. Paul's anger was asking him to pay attention to it, but he hadn't previously been listening closely (mindfully) enough to get clued in.

As Paul learned to listen closely to his thoughts and bodily sensations, he realized how the situation he was in with this other boy and his girlfriend was posing some real (or perceived) threat—to his rigid and perhaps insecure sense of himself as a boyfriend and/or a young man in general.

"I realized that I was the real jackass because I was so caught up in my anger. I may have lost my girlfriend, but I'm not going to lose any more relationships because of it. That would just be stupid."

Nav Check

Are you curious about mindfulness and how it might help? Are you willing to keep exploring how it might work in your life? As we've discussed, mindfulness can be a revolutionary tool for dealing with a number of issues, including anger.

Mindfulness will help you become more aware of the causes, components, look, and feel of your anger (even if you tend to keep your anger inside). And not only does practicing mindfulness make you more aware, it also helps you channel anger toward something healthy.

Check in with your internal navigation system. When it comes to how you're currently managing your feelings of anger, ask yourself, *Am I willing to change?* Pause for a moment, and either in writing or in your head, list the pros and cons of this potential shift in mind-set.

With deep listening into what our minds and bodies have to say about frustrating situations, we get access to info about what is out of whack and in need of attention. It's this mindful listening into our thoughts and bodily reactions that we'll dive into in the next chapter. By learning to bring mindfulness to our inner, hostile experience, we set ourselves up for moving forward without being weighed down by the effects of unchecked anger.

chapter 2

Translating the Language of Anger

In this chapter, we'll explore how to tune into what our minds and bodies are really saying when anger shows up. We'll begin with a look at the angry mind.

Over the course of a day full of situations that trigger your anger (evidence that a parent has gone through your bag, a friend ignoring you, or a teacher giving you a hard time in class, for example), a storm of thoughts run through the mind: *I can't believe he's invading my privacy! Does she think she's too good for me? Mr. Lincoln had better watch out next time he decides to disrespect me in front of the whole class....*

While these thoughts are completely understandable, the drain of these angry impulses—and their disruption to your emotional, physical, and social well-being—suggests that a less intense, more flexible reaction might make a really big difference in your life.

The angry thoughts and mental images can present themselves as very real and in need of immediate expression. "They need to know this right now!" they scream. But think back: How well do things tend to turn out when you get stuck thinking like this? Do these thoughts help or hinder your ability to manage your daily life?

We want to bring flexibility into how you relate to your angry thoughts. Instead of screaming at your mom or dad for snooping, unfriending the fool who ignored you, or exploding at a teacher, try a healthy alternative: a heaping helping of mindfulness. Can you just observe your thoughts, without buying into them as absolute truth or trying to force them away?

This is truly radical, life-changing stuff, and I know it's not easy; I also know it works. So, I promise you: it's worth it!

You can't force thoughts away, particularly ones with big energy behind them. What you can do is build your capacity to serve as a witness to your own thoughts. Can you notice yourself thinking right now? Pause and try it. Can you observe your own inner voice?

The moment you try to do so, you are *mindful* of your thoughts, instead of *being* the thoughts. You get a little distance. Typically, when we think about something we're fired up about, that anger feels very close, as if it's inside us, part of who we are. Mindfulness helps us see the angry thought as what it is: just a thought. Just one of the thousands of thoughts our minds churn out on a daily basis.

Mindfulness practice helps us go behind the impulse and watch our own thinking, to notice thoughts come and go without reacting to them. This sounds simple, and it is. Like bubbles you've blown, thoughts are just there. They float around a bit and eventually drift away and pop.

Mindfulness has the potential to help us pull out of anger's tunnel vision and see things (particularly other people) more clearly. It can even keep us connected to others.

To manage your inner digital assistant, pick up your phone and try the exercises that follow.

Give It a Go: Cell Phone Meditation

1. Sit comfortably, in an upright posture, with your phone in the palm of your hand, which you can rest gently on your lap. Keep your eyes open.

2. Turn your phone on, but don't open any apps. Just let your thumb hover above the screen.

3. Take a full, deep breath into your belly. Notice how your breath enters and leaves your body. For at least thirty seconds, practice just noticing the bodily sensations of your breathing. Even though you're looking at your phone, try to focus on the feeling of your breath coming in and out. If your mind drifts away, no problem. Just gently bring awareness back to your breath.

4. Pay attention to whatever feelings arise, and do your best to label them: "angry," "frustrated," or "tired." Just notice the feelings and name them. See if you can keep your attention lightly connected to the sensations of breathing.

5. Come back to noticing your breathing, and silently ask:

- Is there something about looking at my phone that stirs up feelings?

- Does my phone remind me of someone or something?

- Is it frustrating to be looking at my phone without using it?

Most of us are addicted to our cell phones. What happens to people whose access to their drug is blocked? Anger, for one. Just like anger itself, smartphones (and the Internet, social media, and video games, for example) aren't inherently bad. It's how we manage them that can be harmful.

And just as smartphones have a digital voice (Siri or another all-knowing being), we also have an inner voice—it's our thinking!

Let's do a bit more practice with your phone.

Give It a Go: Smarter Than Your Phone

Call to mind a recent time when you were angry. Imagine the situation in detail, seeing, hearing, and feeling what happened as if it were a movie. If the first scene you think of feels too painful, try another. Go easy on yourself.

Now, out loud to yourself, say quietly what you're thinking about this situation—like this ...

"I'm having the thought that [insert your thought here].*"*

This will help you step back and *watch* the thought. Imagine that it's the voice of your phone. It's trying to give you valuable information, to warn you about something up ahead, or both—maybe even something that's blocking what matters to you.

You don't have to treat the voice as if it's Divine Truth that you must blindly obey. You can simply sit back and watch what your phone is saying. This is very different than trying to force a thought away.

You can mindfully continue to play with the angry thought by trying these approaches:

- Think to yourself, *Thanks, Mind, for coming up with* [insert angry thought].

- Take a breath and picture a mental image of the thought on your phone's screen. Vividly imagine the shape, color, size, movement, and sounds of the thought. Just watch and listen to it; it's just there. Information, not your full reality.

- Ask yourself, *Is there info here that might allow me to make my life better, or easier? Is there something that makes sense to move toward, instead of away from?* You get to decide—not anyone else.

The goal with all these techniques is to shift from a rigid, reactive, black-and-white way of thinking to a more easygoing relationship with your anger. Think of how it feels when you and your bestie hang out—and imagine that you and your anger could get along like that.

Your Own Personal Heaven and Hell

When you get really angry and begin to lose control, you could be in a tropical paradise, and you'd still be in hell. Consider the following fable:

> A powerful samurai warrior happens upon an old wise man meditating in a lovely Zen garden. The warrior thinks he'll amuse himself by teasing the withered man as he sits, eyes closed, by the path.
>
> "Hey there, wise teacher," says the arrogant samurai. "Tell me the nature of heaven and hell."
>
> Without even opening his eyes, the old man says, "Why should I speak to a worthless heap such as yourself?"
>
> The warrior, enraged at the insolence of this old man, draws his sword and raises it overhead, poised to strike the helpless man down. "That's hell," says the teacher, pointing a wrinkled finger at the warrior.
>
> Hearing this, the samurai drops his sword and begins shaking with sobs. "I can't believe what I almost did! I almost murdered this poor man!"
>
> "And that's heaven," the old man says, pointing again at the now-wiser warrior.

You create your own heaven and hell with your thoughts. As a therapist, I've been trained to spot and help people deal with repetitive and negative inner chatter that eats away at minds and bodies from the inside. This sort of thinking (called "rumination"), particularly if it's angry in nature, can really wreck your ability to see things accurately. Your thinking gets in a repetitive loop, stuck in either the past—something that already happened—or the future—what you're going to do about it.

In my case, I can get stuck telling myself that I'm a failure as a therapist if I lose focus on a patient for a split second during a session. Or building a deadly future version of myself, based on a minor insult in a text exchange with a friend. Rumination is the run-on self-talk of the mind, with agitated energy as both its fuel and its output. Ruminative thinking is toxic to our well-being and clarity of mind.

Mindfulness practices can help minimize rumination. Like training a puppy to stay, mindfulness helps our attention stay in the present moment without reacting. Try this next practice and get a sense of what it's like to chill out and get comfy on the couch of the present.

Give It a Go: Your Handheld TimeLESS Machine

1. Stand, placing your phone on the ground in front of you.

2. Put something representing "past" to the left of it, and representing "future" to its right (for example, a receipt from a store from a recent shopping

trip, and an ad for your number-one future travel destination).

3. Now, try to go into the past or future by moving your phone to the left or right, as if it's a mini time machine.

4. Notice that even when you're moving your phone into "past" and "future," it's still here, now, in the present moment. Your phone can't time travel, and neither can you. It, and you, are always in the present moment.

5. Ask yourself, *How often do I look at my phone and get lost in thoughts of the past or the future? What would happen if instead, I remembered that I am always in the present?*

6. Gently bring your attention to the sounds around you. Allow your mind to quiet, letting thoughts pass as you focus on listening. Life is happening all around you; listen for the pieces of it, both near and far. It is all there within the expanse of your mind. Notice how sounds come and go; thoughts might too, but they're mere blips on the great screen of your awareness. Continue in this way for a few minutes, resting in the sounds appearing and disappearing around you.

7. Repeat this practice anytime you want to.

Now, hopefully, you can see more clearly that rumination happens when you forget that they're just thoughts—when you believe you can actually time travel.

Just as you'd likely wreck a car if you drove with your eyes on the screen of your phone, ruminative thinking can wreck your relationships and whatever else is important to you. Your thoughts are happening, but so is everything else. You are more than your thoughts!

Anger sometimes brews when your mind cuts at you, samurai-style, about the past or future. When you ruminate about the past or future, you *become* your anger. Mindfulness helps you stay in the here and now, deal with things directly, connect authentically with others, and get stuff done.

More Than Meets the "I"

How often do you take personally what's happening to you? Do your thoughts make you think that what's happening with your friends, classmates, teachers, coaches, and family is all about *you*, when it likely has little or nothing to do with you at all?

By practicing mindfulness, you start to realize that there's much more than meets the "I." By learning to notice your habit of making everything personal—and by seeing that, in fact, most things that happen to you really don't have anything to do with you—you can learn to see when you're overreacting. Everything just doesn't feel so heavy anymore, and it's a relief.

Give It a Go: Taking the "I" Out of Irritated

1. Pick a recent anger-inducing situation from your daily life. It can be a big deal (like a breakup) or something smaller (like getting rude service at a restaurant).

2. Anchor yourself in your breathing. Feel the sensations of your breath in your body as you inhale and exhale for a few complete breaths.

3. Notice something in your immediate surroundings (perhaps the feel of air on your skin, your feet on the floor, or the tick of a clock). Just silently notice something that is there, now, other than you.

4. Tell the story of this particular episode without using any "self" words (I, me, mine, myself, my). If you're alone, try writing the story down on paper. Set a timer for three minutes and see if you can fully tell the story without any of these words. If you're with someone, try telling them the story without the self words. Have your partner "buzz" you if you use one. See how long you can go into the three minutes without a self word.

5. Notice what it's like to tell the story with your "I's" closed. What's it like to focus on this story in a way that has nothing to do with you and your way of seeing things? What if you focused less on yourself when reacting to frustrating or challenging situations? Would your anger get in the way more, or less?

We can all take a spark from a frustrating situation and ignite it into an inferno of anger with our thinking. It comes down to one word: expectation. You expect your friends to notice the cool things you say and do. You expect your parents to respect you. You expect teachers to cut you some slack. You expect that special someone to meet all your emotional and physical needs. And when the world does not comply ... beware of your wrath.

The bigger the gap between what our thinking says "should" be and what actually shows up in reality, the more likely what started out as mere disappointment or slight discomfort will turn into something seemingly out of control and all-consuming.

It's helpful to begin noticing this expectation-focused thinking. While it's important to have goals and plans for the future, the problem arises when we get locked into a rigid assumption that we'll be happy only if reality aligns with our thoughts. But this doesn't really make sense, because how much do expectations actually change anything around you?

Not at all, right? The only thing that does change things is your ability to actually be cool with the reality of what's happening. The more you can accurately deal with what's actually showing up in your daily life, the more you can engage with your circumstances just as they are—the more you can solve problems, get stuff done, and make things happen.

Is your phone handy? (Of course it is!) Here's another quick practice for getting present (and sidestepping the trap of expectation-laden thinking).

Give It a Go: Tag, You're It!

1. Open up a social media app while holding your phone in front of you. Before getting lost in it, pause for a moment. Close your eyes and breathe slowly and deeply for at least two full cycles of breath.

2. Notice how the afterimage of your phone screen leaves its imprint on your mind. Take another couple of slow, deep breaths with your eyes still closed. Ask yourself, *What am I hoping people have posted?* Take another breath, and just quietly watch what happens in your thoughts. *See* your thoughts without *being* your thoughts.

3. Open your eyes and ask yourself, *What's actually happening here and now?* Look at what's on your phone, in your social media, but be an observer, not a participant. Consider your surroundings as well. Just observe your thoughts, and check in with each of your senses. What's here in this moment? What's something you otherwise would have missed? Let go of any expectations and just hang out with your breathing, and the thoughts or pictures showing up.

4. If you're feeling bold, go into your social media and make a quick post about the present moment you're noticing, without expectations.

Profile in Power: Teen vs. Titan

Frustrated and refusing to accept the Chinese government's deaf ear to more democratic discussion in China, then fourteen-year-old Joshua Wong participated in political protests against the government's decision to allow high-speed trains through the Chinese countryside. He went on to found (along with a classmate) a student activist group called Scholarism and began spreading prodemocracy ideas by way of leaflets in his increasingly antidemocratic home of Hong Kong.

Joshua Wong has been fined, jailed, labeled a threat to the ruling Communist Party, and even beaten for his activism. And yet, he has persisted in speaking out for democratic principles. He didn't just get angry and lash out in unhelpful and destructive ways. He didn't turtle up into hopeless passivity. He turned his anger into a steady, motivated stream of indignation and went after possibilities for change with grit and passion. This teen took on a tyrannical government and brought attention to what otherwise might have been missed by the rest of the world.

Oh, and he was nominated for the Nobel Peace Prize in 2018. Joshua Wong shows us what learning to take the reins of anger can accomplish.

Name It to Tame It

Many centuries ago, the Roman emperor and philosopher Marcus Aurelius said that "the happiness of your life depends upon the quality of your thoughts." On one particular day some years ago, my thoughts were lacking in quality. My nine-month-old daughter had been up for much of the night, leaving my wife and me with only a few hours' sleep. Before we left the house, my wife and I got into an argument about who should've gotten up with the baby during the night.

I was hit by one issue after another as soon as I walked into my office. An upset parent who'd left a voice mail "urgently" needed to talk to me. A supervisee needed help dealing with a crisis. An important meeting I needed to chair, I'd forgotten to put in my calendar. I sat with my face in my hands at my desk, seething with what life had deposited on top of me. My temples were pulsing, and it was only nine thirty.

Somehow, I remembered something I'd recommended to clients many times but usually forgot to do myself. It was a nice therapeutic "nugget" that I called "Name It." You simply say to yourself whatever negative emotion you're experiencing, as you're experiencing it, in order to begin to get some distance from it.

I hesitated. A simple strategy like this one was for my clients to use, I thought—I was an experienced psychologist, beyond such basic techniques. But I was wrong, because as I sat at my desk with frustration shaking through me, I knew I needed to return to the basics.

Research has shown that just labeling negative feelings as they're happening can help people recover control. The brain clicks on its more reasonable thinking centers when we name or label things. Acknowledging our emotions as we're having them seems to put them at arm's length. We can see them, and then we can begin to choose—to open ourselves and connect with others rather than being carried away by a flood of emotional neurochemicals.

Give It a Go: Stinking Thinking

When you find your body and mind hardening with frustration, nudge yourself to attach words to the experience. Using the metaphor of your hand in front of your face can be helpful. Can't see anything, can you?

As you start to label your emotion, creating more and more distance between the raw emotion and you, the frontal lobe of your brain helps you begin to see things more clearly—the hand moves farther away from your face.

Here's an example of a possible progression:

- Frustrating/upsetting event occurs ...

- Body stiffens, clenches ...

- You think, "I can't believe this!" or "They are *so* wrong!" or "This is so messed up!"

- "I'm really angry."

- "My body is telling me I'm ticked off."

- "Anger is here. This is upsetting."

- "Anger ... Anger ... Anger..."

Notice the feeling of the distance that develops as you label your way away from the event, and step away from the raw emotion itself. Instead of reacting and either lashing out or shutting down, in a matter of seconds you can ignite your frontal lobe and choose your response. You can connect with your experience and the possibilities around you. Instead of digging a deeper hole, you can climb out of the one you're in.

Here's another idea for labeling your anger when it shows up: Try attaching a word or two to describe the need of yours that feels trampled on. (Remember RSVP from the introduction? **R**espect, **s**pace, **v**alidation, **p**rovisions, and time with **p**eers.)

Most of us, me included, struggle with distorted, irrational thinking—stinking thinking as I like to call it. When we feel like others are shutting down our needs, we very naturally can get ticked off. But it is our thinking that is out of whack with the facts of reality. We then can get caught up in ruminating, repeating these thoughts to ourselves and getting ourselves more and more worked up. So, try adding a word or two about your patterns of stinking thinking around

- feeling disrespected;

- feeling intruding upon;

- feeling that you or others are wrong or bad; and

- believing that your friends or peers are to blame for your situation, or that they will reject you.

Putting it all together, naming and taming angry thinking might sound like this:

"I'm so ticked off!" ... "I'm having angry thoughts and bodily reactions." ... "Anger is showing up." ... "I'm feeling disrespected." ... "Oh, and I'm playing the blame game." ... "Anger ... anger ... blame ... blame."

You get the idea. Practice this labeling whenever you can. Try not to get discouraged when you find yourself swept away in the emotional currents of anger. Our emotional reflexes run deep, and change comes only with significant practice and patience. Your anger will continue to flare—but you can get better at catching it before it spins out of control.

Give It a Go: Lava Lingo

Sometimes when we're angry, we think certain "not nice" things about others—words that have heat to them, that can burn like lava flowing out of a volcano. This exercise gives you an easy-to-use tool for getting your power back, no matter how "hot" the word is.

1. Think of a recent situation when you were really angry. What specific word or words pop up in your thoughts? Don't censor yourself. You have my permission (as long as this is *your* copy of the book!) to graffiti up the margins of this page with the nasty verbiage that spews forth. Maybe it's a colorful

description for a certain someone, or maybe it's a word that expresses how dark or messed up things feel right now.

2. Now—as long as you're not in the middle of a religious service or a math lecture—say the word(s) aloud, over and over as fast as you can for at least thirty seconds. Say them so fast that you almost can't get them out. Go!

3. Notice what happens after you've done this. Do the words still have the same power they had? Are they still as hot as lava? Who has control over how you feel—these words or you?

The power of lava lingo is knowing when to use it. (Tip: it also works if you just say the words silently to yourself.) If you do this consistently and with the intention of cooling off, you will likely find it really refreshing.

Real Talk: Sophie's Stinking Thinking

Fifteen-year-old Sophie is angry at the teachers at her school (and may have good reasons to be).

"People just need to leave me alone. Every adult at school is just there to get a paycheck, and they are always assuming I did it when something goes wrong or gets messed up. Sure, I do stuff, but that doesn't give them the right to send me out of the room before I've even told my side of things. I think my physics teacher in particular is looking to screw me over on purpose—get me suspended or something. Anger is for the better. I get yelled at by everyone, it seems like. I've just learned to tell all these adults to back off. I like to yell back and get them upset. So yeah, I get angry, very angry. It works out for me."

Mind-set Reset

Do you think Sophie's expectations help or hinder her daily life? How is her thinking hooking her and fueling her anger?

Remember, our ruminations, our habits of tunnel vision, though they might feel like they're there to protect us, actually often trip us up. With habits of mindfulness—about what's actually happening around her (and inside her)—Sophie can begin to get clear on what her anger is really about. She can then start making different choices and creating different outcomes in her daily life at school and in general.

Here's what she had to say after learning to listen more mindfully to her anger:

"Little did I know, anger is a short-term solution that can lead to some pretty long-term problems. Anger is completely possessive. It doesn't like sharing the mind with any other emotion and most definitely doesn't play well with others. It is consuming and comforting, and usually gives me a way to justify my actions.

"This tough facade I was putting up did not allow me to sustain meaningful relationships. I was starting to realize that if you don't make yourself vulnerable to people, how are they supposed to trust you? The first step was realizing I wanted to change. The second step was accepting what already was. I learned to love the angry parts of myself because those parts had practically saved me. I also learned I didn't need to keep rejecting people before they could ever get the chance to reject me."

Nav Check

As you read through this chapter, did you find yourself noticing your anger-related thoughts more? What was it like to see these thoughts, without attaching to them so closely—essentially *becoming* them?

In the next chapter, we will shift from getting mental to getting physical. In order to harness your anger, it's crucial that you listen closely to the messages your thoughts give regarding what's missing, failed, or in jeopardy in your life. But you can also get good intel from your body. Your physical body is giving you subtle and not-so-subtle hints as to what's out of tune that may be leading to your anger. We will begin to learn how to read these clues, to tune into the truth of what your body is trying to tell you.

chapter 3

Feeling It to Heal It

What would it be like if you never felt any physical pain? Sounds good, right? There's actually a very rare genetic disorder (congenital insensitivity to pain with anhidrosis, or CIPA for short) that is a pretty terrifying situation, especially for parents of young kids, who live in fear of their children severely (or fatally) injuring themselves because their bodies don't send them the messages of physical pain that you and I take for granted. These pain messages prompt us to pull back from threatening things in the world, and they keep us safe.

It's similar with emotional pain. We need the pain of sadness, fear, disgust—and yes, anger—to wake us up and prompt us to take action. But many of us spend far too much time in our heads (or on our phones) and less and less time listening to the important messages the body and mind are sending. Even though the tech coming at us at a faster and faster pace has its upside, the downside is that we're becoming increasingly disconnected from our bodies—the greatest tech of all.

The human body gives us an amazingly sensitive "receiver" (by way of our senses) for what's going on around us that matters. It also provides a potent vehicle with which to leave our mark on the world. How many of your devices have this much power? (And come to you free of charge! Not even a monthly subscription fee.) But unlike your devices, or that Lego kit you used to have, your body does not come with a set of detailed instructions.

That's where this book comes in. You can learn to use the tech the universe has given you, to not only get on top of your anger but also ride it all the way toward your greatest potential.

If you're not currently angry about something, don't worry— we're going to get you there. Why not poke the bear a bit?

Give It a Go: Rage Across the Page

Think of a recent situation that got you seriously annoyed: That guy who keeps harassing your girlfriend (or sister), or that teacher who keeps sticking it to you. Perhaps a friend stole the spotlight and is getting all the credit for something you did. Whatever it is, let yourself think about it—better yet, feel the full-throated, fists clenched, red-in-the face physical side of your anger. Go ahead, let 'er rip!

Now grab a pen or pencil along with a journal, a notebook, or even a takeout menu if need be, and let loose your rage! Write or draw as fast or as slow as you want to. Pour your anger onto the page just as it is without censoring it. Let loose and charge yourself up. Definitely don't worry about staying inside the lines.

Now, let's pause for a quick mindfulness exercise.... Don't put the book down!

Give It a Go: SLOW Breathing

In order to really listen to what your anger has to teach you, you can use your breathing as a sort of scope, like the ones doctors use, to go inside and see the fine print of what's happening. To do that, let's practice—after getting all worked up—slowing down your mind and body so that you can keep yourself in check.

At each step, pause for a moment to actually *feel* the body part fully, as you let your breathing guide you down into your body. Let any tension or clenching there loosen up/go slack before moving on.

1. **S**top—Stop what you are doing. Inhale slowly and deeply into your belly. Imagine that the air is circulating in and around the muscles of your face, creating tiny spaces there, loosening and slackening. Feel and soften the muscles of your face for at least ten seconds. Breathe slowly and let your face muscles go slack and loose.

2. **L**ower—Take another slow belly breath and lower your shoulders. Imagine your shoulders deflating as you breathe, going flat like balloons losing their air. Focus on the sensations of your shoulders for at least ten seconds. Breathe and let your shoulders lower and loosen.

3. **O**pen—With your breath, open your chest and belly, deeply feeling the rise and fall of sensations in your belly for at least ten seconds. Breathe slowly and deeply down into your belly, letting it expand and open.

4. **W**ilt—Breathe in again and imagine your breath going all the way down into your hands, your fingers. Feel the sensations of your fingertips for at least ten seconds. Like a plant or flower left out in the sun too long, allow your fingers to "wilt," to go limp. Let your hands and fingers go loose.

With practice, SLOW breathing can bring you more fully into your body. It can help you find ease and calm in the middle of a test at school, at home when your parents are fighting, or at work when your boss is in a bad mood. SLOW breathing is a tool for exploring what's happening in your body *and* for bringing your body into a softer, slower, more receptive state.

You can't really notice what's going on inside you if you aren't able to receive information. That's why it's so important to learn to stay with the physical discomfort—the tense, rigid, hot, surging, pulsing sensations of anger. As we'll see later in this section, once you can hang out with the physical side of anger (listening to your angry thoughts without *being* them), you can begin to listen into what your body may be storing below the anger.

Are you still a little charged up from your rage writing or drawing? Here's another quick body-based exercise; another tool for slowing the body down so that you can actually hear what it has to say. And by the way, this and the previous exercise can also help you steer clear of some of the trouble you may have gotten into in the past.

Give It a Go: Math Breath

This one's simple and, with practice, can be powerful in reining in the extremes of your anger. It's just a simple formula: $5 + 3 = 8$.

1. Breathe in slowly to the count of five.

2. Pause and gently hold your breath to the count of three.

3. Slowly breathe out to the count of eight.

That's it! Give it a shot now.

You don't have to like math for this exercise to come in handy in a stressful situation. A job interview perhaps? Just before you're about to ask that hottie out for a date?

It also helps you to get clear in order to hear the messages of your body.

Having an "In the Body" Experience

In this section, we'll explore how anger shows up physically in your body. With the mindful breathing tools you've just learned, you're ready for an expedition inside.

Remember our AMPed-up definition of mindfulness (**a**ware of the **m**oment at hand as it **p**lays itself out without judging)? Instead of your anger spinning you out of control with aggression, what if you could bring mindfulness into your anger, to not only learn to manage it but also to slide behind it and find out what it might be covering up?

Anger is often a protective shield against other painful feelings. But if you're not paying close attention, you can get lost in the anger and miss the other stuff underneath.

Recent science has helped create a visual map of how emotions tend to manifest in the body. The map varies a bit from person to person, but each of the major emotions (including anger, of course) has a sort of signature—a certain area of the body where we tend to experience that specific emotion.

But before I reveal the treasure map, try your hand at it first. Artistic talent not required.

Give It a Go: Body Map

In a journal or notebook, draw a quick outline that represents your body.

Next, take a minute and draw or shade in where you feel anger in your own body. Be as specific as possible. If one area usually feels more intense with anger than another, you can shade it in darker. If an area feels "sharp," maybe you can draw lines or edges to give it this quality. Be creative and be as detailed as possible. Don't worry about being wrong. The way anger shows up for you might clue you in to some good intel—so listen closely.

Now, put your pen or pencil down and close your eyes. Begin the slow, deep belly breathing you did in the SLOW scan, or math breathing. Be curious and listen into your body. Where, *specifically*, do you feel the breath in your body? Try to notice even the subtlest sensations. Listen for heat, stiffness, pulsing, prickling, or even numbness. Don't judge or analyze your sensations, but simply collect them like a scientist. Note or draw the sensations of your breathing in your journal or notebook.

Now, along with these very small, specific sensations in your body, choose a picture, symbol, or specific word that's important to you: that makes you think of being grounded, or safely connected. Choose something that matters to you, resonates with you. Imagine that the sensations in your body are like one side of a piece of Velcro, and your word, symbol, or mental picture is the other side of the Velcro. Imagine sticking them together. This Velcro will anchor your breathing from now on; your attention can "stick" to it. For SLOW scans, math breathing, or any deep, calming breath, you can anchor your attention to these sensations along with this mental image or word. And right now as I'm writing this sentence, I can notice the sensations of my breath passing over my upper lip as I think the words "awesome sauce!" to myself. Try *not* paying attention to that!

When you AMP up your attention, you're allowing mindfulness to seep into the deeper crevices of your body and mind. Most of us go about our day on autopilot and don't notice the quieter (and sometimes more uncomfortable) sensations of sadness, fear, shame, and loss. Anger is easy to notice, because of its drama-queen tendencies. It devours all our attention. But even as it might be trying to protect us from deeper, quieter pain, it actually doesn't allow that pain to move—it instead stays stuck inside our bodies and minds.

Mindfulness is like a slow, yet steady drip of water that starts with a trickle and, if you keep it up, will eventually will wash the pain through and out of you.

So now, the big reveal. Research suggests that many people tend to feel anger in the face, throat, and chest—but if you don't happen to, don't worry. It's different for everyone. The point here is that wherever you feel anger showing up, there are usually subtler, softer, quieter sensations behind the bodily sensations of anger. Now you have some intel as to what these other sensations are, and you're perhaps also a bit curious as to what they mean. Perhaps they're remnants—the echoes of pains such as sadness, loss, resentment, loneliness; there are many possibilities. Now, you have some more information to work with, and you may actually start getting a better sense of what you might need to do to get your life going in a more powerful direction.

Should I Stay or Should I Go?

It's important for you to learn to hang out with your uncomfortable emotions, in order to get accurate information to solve your problems, help you connect with others, and move toward meaningful pursuits.

It's also important for you to learn when to allow yourself to back away from focusing in on really intense, painful emotions. Mindfulness practice is not meant as a tool for torturing yourself. As country singer Kenny Rogers used to sing, "You have to know when to hold 'em and know when to fold 'em." His song may have been about playing poker, but it can be applied to managing intense emotions as well. The Clash also sang "Should I Stay or

Should I Go?" Their song was about a love relationship, but the lyrics may feel appropriate to this process of discernment: "If I go there will be trouble, but if I stay it will be double."

Yes, in order to really get on top of your anger, you need to learn to hang out with and listen to it and other negative emotions. Sometimes when it's really intense, the most skillful thing to do is to stay only as long as is comfortable, then shift away if you need to focus on something else that's important in the moment, or to keep yourself from getting completely overwhelmed or out of control.

Here, we'll practice both staying with and moving away from the sensations of anger.

Give It a Go: Tsunami Surfing

Anger can hit us like a tsunami. Instead of getting knocked over by it, what if we could learn to surf it—to ride it out with skillful balance? If you can learn to do this, you can see where the flow might take you (and possibly learn about the other negative feelings that might be churning beneath, like sadness or fear).

1. Sit comfortably, upright on a chair or cushion.

2. Listen into your breath. Don't change it. Just notice how it feels going in and out of your body. Notice where in your body you feel it—the bodily-sensation side of the Velcro in the exercise above.

3. Notice your thoughts (even thoughts like *I can't do this*). Notice any other emotions, sensations, or even

memories that pop up—and where you feel these in your body.

4. Focus on one area of the body where you can feel the sensations of anger, and notice how it feels. Notice where it is, its size, where it begins and ends, how intense it is, and even how big it feels. Notice and be curious about how this might change as you continue to breathe in and out. Listen in so closely that you can notice as the sensations shift and change on their own. Repeat this with each part of your body where you notice anger.

5. Keep watching the anger in your body as it rises and falls like a wave in the ocean. Hang ten, surfer-friend!

If you are not angry at the moment, try standing up right now and doing twenty rapid jumping jacks. Now see what's there. Be sure to listen into the feelings closely enough that you can stay balanced as they rise, crest, and fall.

It's really hard to have an accurate view of what's on the beach, or even what's in the water with you, if you're off your board, flailing away and getting trounced by a big wave. Surfing (that is, staying with) the sensations of anger gives you a vantage point for seeing things more clearly (and dealing with them more effectively).

Give It a Go: Icing Your Anger

Here's another one for staying with and seeing behind anger. Between the stressors of homework, friend drama, sports— let alone all the fun stuff at home—teens these days have many opportunities to work with anger! This activity will help you get some practice melting into it in order to emerge into greener pastures. Enough metaphor; let's practice!

1. Set a timer for between three and five minutes.

2. Get an ice cube and sit in a quiet place. Hold the cube in an open hand and simply look at it. Breathe deeply and slowly, letting the air fill your belly.

3. Notice all the sensations in your hand. Stinging, burning, pulsing—whatever is there, if you can just feel it without moving or doing anything. Just like with the feelings of anger that show up in your body, see if you can listen into the sensations and hang out for a while.

4. Hold the ice without dropping it or setting it down before the timer stops. What do you notice? Does your brain tell you to drop it, or throw it away? What's happening to the ice, without you doing anything? Are things changing? Keep up your deep, slow breathing.

In this activity, you have to deal with something physically challenging. Sometimes anger is like that. We get upset, our bodies get tense, and we walk around hardened and emotionally prickly. We may even try to force the discomfort away by blaming or taking it out on others, or numbing out with substances, or social media tirades.

Here you've learned that if you pause and listen into the sensations of anger in your body and the thoughts passing by, anger (like a melting ice cube) can and will change on its own. And if you let the anger change, it might give way enough to reveal feelings that have been tucked away and neglected from healing so that you can get your life on a better track.

When you're getting flooded, feeling out of control of your impulses, or on the verge of lashing out, regardless of the potential consequences, it's not the time to try to merely listen into your anger. You may need to actively move your attention away from the bodily sensations of anger and focus on getting things under control. Let's practice shifting *away* from the physical sensations of anger.

Give It a Go: Hot Coal

This activity will help you notice how temporary the physical sensations of anger are and help create room for skillfully managing this discomfort and getting curious about the quieter echoes of sadness, shame, or loss lying dormant underneath. By learning to not immediately shove the sensations of anger away, you might learn something about the deeper message anger is sending about these subterranean dwellers.

For this, you'll need a small pebble (or a marble), a shoe, and an open mind.

1. Set a timer for three to five minutes. Take in a slow breath, inhaling into your belly. Exhale fully and then notice how you feel. Take a mental snapshot of how you're feeling overall.

2. Place the pebble in your shoe and sit with both feet flat on the floor. Lightly press your foot against the pebble. Notice the pressure and discomfort, and press until it is only moderately uncomfortable. (Don't overdo it!) If you're willing, try standing up and taking a few steps with it in your shoe.

   If you had to walk around like this the rest of today, how would you be feeling by the end of the day? If this pebble was your feeling of anger (a "hot coal") over some upsetting conversation or interaction, how would it affect you to walk around stepping on it all day? Would you ignore it, or be triggered all day and lash out at anyone who came near?

3. Sit back down and resume only a moderate degree of pressure against the pebble with your foot. Now draw your focus and attention to the feeling of your breath—the sensations of your breathing, wherever you feel them most strongly in your body (nostrils, throat, or belly). Rest your attention on these sensations. If you happen to be drawn away by the sensations of discomfort in your foot, simply acknowledge them. Say to yourself something like, *Hey angry foot! I feel you there. Excuse me, but I'm going to*

go back to what I'm focusing on right now (that is, your sensations of breathing). Let yourself lightly notice the pulse of discomfort, and then come back to your breathing.

4. Continue to gently direct your attention back from your foot (or any other distraction) to the feeling of your breathing, as many times as necessary until the timer sounds.

5. After the timer sounds, take another snapshot of how you feel overall.

Which way of relating to your "hot coal" felt best: walking around and trying to ignore it, lashing out at the world as a way of expressing it, or saying hi to it and gently coming back to the feeling of your breath? Which allowed you the most freedom to move about without getting swamped vby the discomfort?

We can't always control something that shows up to irritate and anger us. What's most important is how we learn to relate to what shows up *inside* us—the thoughts and bodily sensations.

Were you willing to notice the pain of the pebble against your foot and come back to what mattered—your breath? What if someone had ticked you off during first period, and instead of trying to either ignore what happened, or thinking about it nonstop, you gently noticed the angry sensations and came back to what you really wanted to focus on?

In the next session, we take things a bit deeper. We're on the hunt for hidden sources of your anger that may be tucked away inside your body.

The Body Never Forgets

When it comes to pain and discomfort, it makes sense that we usually want to steer clear. Pain = bad, and pleasure = good, right? It's not that I'm disagreeing—I like pleasure and dislike pain as much as anyone. When it comes to anger though, the issue is that the bodily sensations of anger are usually just what's on the surface—what's loudest, easiest to recognize.

Often (but not always), anger is a hard crust covering up the deeper, more painful, more vulnerable feelings inside. Sometimes, anger is a basic, pure reaction to what matters to us being threatened—a surge of energy in the body, protecting our safety and self-interest by nudging us to take action. Nothing wrong with that! Pure, clean anger is usually temporary and can give us a jolt of motivation that can help us. It's the anger that plays dirty—stained and muddied up by our overthinking (and distorting) minds—that gets us in trouble.

Some people lash out when their feelings of loss and sadness get too intense (after someone dies or rejects them, or they're traumatized in some way). Some lash out at themselves (and others) when the shame of their failures becomes unbearable. Some shut down when depression and fear become overwhelming, their minds stuck saying that things are hopeless and will never get better.

Anger can help us by temporarily distracting our bodies and minds from these deeper discomforts, but the body never forgets. The body simply stores away the pain and tension inside. In this way, your body never lies—it tells you the story of the painful lessons in your past. Chronic aches and pains are sometimes more than a mere inconvenience: They can be your body knocking at your door, asking you to open up and give them some air.

This is why it's so important to "listen" closely to the truths your body tells. For example, we've all gotten "hangry" at times—research even shows that we see the world more negatively when we're experiencing hunger pangs. But if we're not paying close attention to the true source of our bodily discomfort—our empty bellies—we can let our emotions rush to anger. This is where AMPing up our attention with mindfulness can help. We can learn to practice placing our attention on the moment at hand as it plays out (without judging and overthinking).

Let's use our daily physical experience of hunger to explore this a bit. If you learn to read the cues of hunger in your body, you can sidestep behaving hangrily with others. It's a good place to practice AMPing up your attention, to later apply the same process to other physical sensations, to learn about what they, too, are saying.

Give It a Go: Hangry Helper

The next time you notice you're hungry, before you run to fill that hole with a snack, pause instead, and try the following.

1. Sit down, close your eyes and ask, *Where exactly is "hunger" expressing itself in my body? What are the sensations, and where do I feel them?*

2. When you think you've identified the "what" and "where" of your hunger, stop and listen even more closely. What else and where else? Sit quietly and

listen for more sensations. What messages is your body giving you? It's telling you what it needs. Do more sensations show up, the more you listen?

3. Ask other W questions: When is your hunger? (Why are these sensations happening now? Has it just been a while since you ate, or is something else cuing them?) Why is your hunger? (Is your body truly saying it needs fuel—or is it telling you to eat so that you don't have to think or feel other, more unpleasant things?)

Here's an important principle for you to ponder when it comes to relating to your anger: Sensations in your body are not just a result of the environment. Our bodies don't just passively react to the world bumping up against them. With our minds, we actively *create* sensations inside our bodies.

Pure anger may flash when you're riding your bike on a busy street and a car cuts you off—the driver just threatened your safety. But when the mind starts playing dirty—*That asshole did that on purpose! Screw you, dude!*—the bodily sensations can go from a flash of pure anger (to motivate a safety response) to a draining onslaught of hours (or even days) of tension, headache, and agitation. The mind has created sensations that were not directly caused by this bad driver—sensations that are avoidable, if you stay aware.

It takes really listening into both the body and the mind as they dance with each other. When you listen closely, you can notice the small gaps where you can insert some new, more graceful steps to lead things in a healthier, more effective direction.

Let's practice listening into the body a little more, to learn what else it has to say about anger.

Give It a Go: Sensation Seeker

With this activity, we're going to assume exaggerated body postures and notice how the body responds: how the mind tends to either skip over these sensations or rush to judgment about them.

The goal here is to notice every sensation in your body. Anger tends to snatch our attention—often in order to help us deal with perceived threats. The downside is that it can make it hard to notice the deeper feelings underneath, which really need some air time.

1. Stand as tall as possible. Reach your hands to the sky or ceiling and stretch. Come up onto your toes if possible. Now flatten your feet on the floor, puff out your chest, and make your body as firm and solid as possible. How does this feel? Hold the posture and really pay attention to how it feels internally and emotionally. Do you feel weak or powerful? Open or closed up? Don't try to make something up; instead, just practice noticing whatever it is that shows up. Simply seek out the sensations without trying to force anything.

2. Curl yourself up into a ball on the floor—the fetal position, or maybe child's pose in yoga. Try not to

clench or grip yourself tightly; go as loose and limp as possible. Listen for what your body says about how this position feels. How is it the same or different than standing tall?

3. Now stand up and begin swaying and jumping around randomly. Start slow and get loose and wild as you go. Don't worry about how you look—move in whatever way feels right, but do so rapidly and with a lot of energy. (Check the space first, for pets, younger siblings, or rare Ming dynasty vases in your vicinity!) Now pause and notice all your body's sensations. Don't analyze or judge them—just listen into what your body is saying.

The body has all kinds of sensations popping up all the time, but we tend to miss most of them. We're too much in our heads too much of the time. We're too preoccupied with our important thoughts and mental pictures to really hear what the body is saying. Think how you feel when you're ignored—this might help you feel compassion for your body and to better understand it. The brain is like an overperforming older sister, constantly hogging the limelight.

The more you listen, the more your body will tell you its truth. You might hear faint echoes of sadness, worry, fear, or loss. They need your full attention. Anger keeps drowning them out!

Profile in Power: Healing Hate

In October 2012, a fourteen-year-old girl was riding in a school van in Mingora, Pakistan, when an armed terrorist jumped into the van and shot her in the head. She had been targeted by Taliban terrorists for having spoken out publicly about education reform—particularly for girls, who are often denied an education—in Pakistan. Her name is Malala Yousafzai, and not only did she survive this attack and recover from her wounds, but she went on to win the Nobel Peace Prize for her activism before and after this attack.

The Taliban terrorists thought that attacking Malala would silence her, and others like her. But not only is the now twenty-year-old Malala still speaking—her voice has grown in power and influence as she travels the world, spreading her message of education and peace for women and for all Pakistanis.

In March 2018, Malala returned to Pakistan for the first time since being shot. As she spoke, she cried, and the crowd broke out in applause. "I was always dreaming for the past five years that I can come to my country, whenever I was traveling abroad. Finally, I am here."

Malala Yousafzai experienced excruciating physical and emotional pain from the trauma of the near-fatal attack and the ongoing threat to her life. She has not allowed the pain to flood her with hate, however. Her anger has been converted into a powerful, persistent drive to use her voice for change—much further than anyone (including her) could ever have anticipated six years prior.

Your Inner Frenemy

Ancient Chinese military scholar and philosopher Sun Tzu wrote, "Keep your friends close and your enemies closer." He was advising warlords of the fifth century BCE to keep close tabs on the opposition—even to the point of fostering alliances with them.

It's good advice. But in this context, your enemy isn't the boss in your video game or your English teacher who just doesn't get you. It's the feelings of discomfort and outright pain that you hold in your body, imprisoned under layers of mean, distorted anger. This enemy is far more powerful because it's *in you*, and it's actually the most insightful teacher you'll ever know. The feelings and sensations that are covered up by the heat and tension of anger are there to teach you—but that can happen only if you let yourself see and feel them.

Ask yourself, *Would everyone who experiences what I experience have the same degree of anger I do in reaction to certain people or situations?* No, right? If others would relate to these people or situations differently, what does this suggest?

Let's go to an emotional boot camp of sorts, to see if we can sort this out.

Give It a Go: Shadow Boxing

In the world of boxing, punches are often taught in the form of combinations—for example, a jab, a hook, and an uppercut in quick sequence, a one-two-three to defeat your opponent.

Let's go a few rounds against your mind and body, to see if we can get beneath the anger—to the real threat to you.

1. Think of a recent situation in which *one* person sparked an insane amount of anger for you.

2. Talk out loud (to yourself, the mirror, a trusted friend, or in writing) about the thing this person did that was deserving of your anger.

3. Now talk or write as if that other person was in the room with you right now—just the *two* of you—and you're talking directly to them about what they did.

4. Now look in a mirror (or your reflection in your phone) and talk, or think, to yourself about *three* things inside your body that you are sensing or feeling right now. Really listen, patiently, for messages of discomfort or outright pain; they may appear small and subtle beneath your anger: A quiet pulse of sadness around your eyes and throat. A shudder in your gut signaling fear or apprehension. A flush in your cheeks suggesting shame.

If nothing shows up, don't sweat it! Just keep listening the next time you feel like giving someone a one-two-three punch combination. Aim to get past the *one* ridiculous thing the other person did on purpose, deeper than how you'd like to blast them if the *two* of you could face off, and look for *three* things lingering inside you that need to start getting some air.

When these deeper pains are felt and released, there's less need for a big pile of anger to cover them up. You're nearing the edge of yourself, where you can look out at the world with much greater clarity.

Real Talk: Mike's Mayhem

Sixteen-year-old Mike had been trying daily mindfulness practices (on the way to school, during homeroom, before starting homework, and before bed). He'd been listening into his body and had noticed quite a lot happening—an inner fireworks show that he'd been covering up with his angry outbursts.

Listen as he tells you how he brought mindful attention to how anger showed up in his body, so that he could go deeper into the painful sources of his anger that he'd been steering clear of.

"I feel my anger in my arms and in my shoulders. Everything tenses and gets ready for this unnecessarily unavoidable, unrealistic battle of wits or fists. It makes me feel powerful and yet out of control. It's kind of addicting, but somehow you know it's bad for you. But in the moment, you just don't care."

Mind-set Reset

Can you see how it might be hard for Mike to simply let go of his anger? It gives him power and energy—if there were nothing in it for him, he would have given it up a long time ago!

Mike needed to learn to listen to his anger as though he were in a relationship with it. And just as with any relationship, there was both a mental and a physical part he needed to relate to. Neglect either part and you're cruising for a relationship disaster.

"The thing about anger is that it's cost me a lot. I've given a lot of myself to the all-consuming power of anger. Most of high school has been defined by it. I've been sad and depressed, and the only way I knew to deal with it was with anger. I've lost friendships, respect, trust, and there have been times that I felt like I'd even lost myself."

Mike learned to have a full, healthy relationship with his anger. He listened to his thoughts and his body; he developed a pretty accurate understanding of what anger had given him and what it had taken away. Once he used mindfulness practices to be more aware of the anger in his mind and body, his attention seeped deeper into his feelings of sadness and loneliness. Now that he's on the road to healing, he's likely going to have more energy for what he truly wants to do in his life—energy that had, before, been drained away by his anger.

We all make our best decisions about our most important relationships when we have all the information we need—when we see our thoughts and physical reactions through the lens of our mindful awareness so that we can give things a long, hard, healthy look.

Nav Check

Anger is self-protection from the perception of threat. The problem is that our perceptions can often be distorted by the complexities of our modern world. This chapter focused on helping you truly listen into and beyond how anger shows up in your body and mind.

Have you ever stacked dominoes and then tipped over the one on the end and watched them fall? Well, that's what our habits of anger are like: thoughts and feelings knocking into one another, gathering momentum, and making a mess of our lives.

Mindfulness skills give you a little space between the thoughts—you can start to hear them without *being* them. If you create more space between stacked dominoes, eventually the cascade stops. The gap allows the habit train of angry reactions to come to a peaceful stop.

You didn't choose to have all these dominoes stacked against you. And yet this is your life. Only you are responsible for learning how to break these patterns. Mindfulness of your thinking can certainly help, and so can mindfulness of your body.

Now that you're listening more carefully to what your mind and body have to say about anger (and you're getting a glimpse of the neglected stuff underneath it), you're ready to start actively seeking a new direction for your actions when you're frustrated or stressed out. This direction will give you more ground to stand on in your daily life.

Part 2

Look for Your Power

chapter 4

The Truth Inside Anger

A frequently repeated story (author unknown) is of a little boy who had a bad temper. His father gave him a bag of nails and told him that every time he lost his temper, he had to hammer a nail into the back of the fence. On the first day, the boy drove thirty-seven nails into the fence. Over the next few weeks, as he learned to get a handle on his anger, the number of nails he hammered daily gradually lessened. He discovered it was easier to hold his temper than to drive those nails into the fence.

Finally, the day came when the boy didn't lose his temper at all. He told his father, who suggested that the boy now pull out one nail for each day that he was able to stay on top of his anger. The days passed, and the young boy was finally able to tell his father that all the nails were gone.

The father took his son by the hand and led him to the fence. He said, "You have done well, my son, but look at the holes in the fence. The fence will never be the same. When you say things in anger, they leave a scar just like this one. You can put a knife into a man and draw it out. It won't matter how many times you say I'm sorry—the wound is still there."

The little boy then understood how powerful his father's words were. He looked up at his father and said, "I hope you can forgive me, Father, for the holes I put in you."

"Yes, I can," the father said.

If you're this far into the book, you've listened closely to your mind and body and have perhaps opened all sorts of unread messages your anger has been sending. Now you're ready for the second stage: looking at your relationships, at what is happening in your daily life. You can get perspective, assess the situation, and get ready to act (the action will happen in part 3).

The story about the nails is not meant to make you feel ashamed of how your anger may have caused damage to you and others in the past. Just the opposite. If you care enough to read this book, you're ready to listen to the truth of your anger, and to look deeply at what matters for you and for others in your life.

In listening beneath the mental and physical surges of anger, you might have heard the rumblings of sadness, worry, and distress. It's here that we'll take the next step—looking. Looking honestly at what's there will support you in channeling your anger toward one of two productive pathways. On the way, we'll take special care to avoid the blame-and-shame trap, which only makes things worse. Instead, you can pause at regret and work toward repairing any hurt you may have caused.

In the future, instead of lashing out and creating more drama for yourself and others, you can channel your anger. Imagine easing your thumb over the mouth of a spouting water hose: the water will spurt out more directly, and you can aim it toward something that needs a good dousing. By looking with mindfulness and clarity at the world around you after getting angry, you can learn to use your anger as fuel. You can ignite it in service of something that needs fixing out in the world.

Before blasting off, though, you need to keep listening. Next, we'll begin looking at the truth of what's really happening. It's time to get real.

The Whole Truth, and Nothing But the Truth

Most of us would agree that we want and need honesty in our relationships with others. Particularly in our closest relationships, a willingness to tell the truth is key to minimizing pain and maximizing understanding.

And by truth, I'm not talking about some mystical parting of clouds and declarations shining down from heaven. I'm not even referring to what most people focus on when talking about honesty in relationships: the absence of lying. No, I'm focused on big "T" truth that is always accurate, can never be dismissed or argued away, and is always available. I'm referring to the truth of our present-moment experience—the truth that arises in the middle of our interactions.

Ask yourself:

- Have I ever felt angry or resentful and yet told someone I was fine when asked?

- Have I ever stayed quiet about a close friend's unhealthy or risky choices even though every fiber of my body was screaming out with dread?

- Have I ever snapped, pushed, pulled, or shut down with someone and said it was something about *them* that was the problem? Have I put blame on another person without saying or doing anything about how I was mismanaging myself in that moment?

- Have I ever said yes when my strong gut feeling was no—or vice versa?

Few of us tell the full truth about anything on a consistent basis, particularly in our close relationships, where there's a lot at stake. We hedge, hide, and flail about with colleagues, family members, and friends—even though we may not be lying in a literal sense. Our brains are biologically wired for snap judgments and rapid emotional reactions in order to help us manage threats—an ancient form of self-protection that served us well in our cave-dwelling days, but that in the modern world is usually more than what's needed.

For example, when I explained to my loved ones, in my early twenties, that law school was not a good fit for me, that the way things were being taught wasn't necessarily the ideal way for me to learn, I was *not* telling the truth of my actual, present-moment experience.

The full truth was that I was terrified, full of self-doubt, and riddled with shame for having "failed." I felt the bodily sensations of anxiety and self-loathing on a daily basis, and my failure and fear of rejection had a choke hold on me.

Not only was this full truth absent from my conversations with loved ones, but I blamed professors, fellow students, and even my family and friends for my predicament. My speech and actions were not connected with my actual experience.

This is where mindfulness can be extremely helpful. When we're surging with discomfort and emotional pain, we need to listen (into) our thoughts and feelings, and then look (out at) our full experience of the world. When we do, we have a shot at saying and doing things skillfully, and perhaps getting ourselves unstuck.

We All Lie Sometimes

Each and every one of us lies about one or more of the following things during communication:

- Our bodies (sensations and emotions)

- Our thoughts

- Our core needs

Again, we lie not because we're bad, but because we experience rapid, reactive blaming and bias toward others as threatening to our well-being, and this perception has helped us stay alive and thrive as a species in the past. Although we are bound to the same biology of our ancestors, with mindfulness we have a shot at slowing down our anger, sidestepping bias and blaming, and cultivating compassionate speech and action. And mindfulness has been experimentally proven to change our brains in measurable and meaningful ways.

Mindfulness gives us a small gap in our minds, a place where we can let the full truth seep in. Remember, with mindfulness we're AMPing up—we're **a**ware of the **m**oment at hand by letting it **p**lay out (without judging or overthinking) in some way.

Let's pause and take a crack at a "truth-telling" practice I use in my work as a psychologist with families, couples, parents, and teens—and with myself. We all fall short of the freedom and ease that can flow from more consistent mindfulness in our communication—the full truth that, without mindful listening and looking, tends to go unaddressed and unarticulated.

Give It a Go: Listening for Truth

1. Before, during, or right after a conflict with someone, pause for a moment. As we've practiced before, listen into the sensations of anxiety, discomfort, or frustration that are showing up in your body. Listen with curious, compassionate attention. Breathe into and penetrate them. See the truth of them—a truth that is direct and undeniable.

2. Slowly tighten your right hand into a fist. Draw your attention to the sensations there in your hand. Imagine all the tension, clenching, or surging in your body gravitating to the sensations in your fist. This entire practice may last only a few breaths, but notice how rapidly and readily you can direct your attention to this one area of your body. Breathe into the tension in your hand. You get to choose exactly

---

when to focus in on these sensations, which ones to zoom in on, and how long you hang out "listening" to them. Basically, you get to choose how you *relate* to this tension in your body.

3. Now let go of the tension in your right hand and open it, palm up. Now you're looking—you're noticing how the sensations in your hand change. Watch how you can let go of being "right" and just witness the truth of what both your body and thoughts are saying. No need to grab onto anything—just look at things clearly and let it all be as it is.

4. And now with a final deep breath, ask yourself, *As I look at what is happening inside and around me, what matters most to me in this moment? What do I need? What is simply not right about what others have done, or what I've done?* Perhaps it's respect or even honesty itself that you want or need. Consider saying it out loud.

5. And finally, ask yourself, *Am I willing to speak from the full truth of what the listening and looking are showing me? Am I willing to let my wild anger become a focused laser—a source of fuel for taking actions that help change what's not right about myself or in the world?*

These tips can help make this exercise as powerful as possible:

- Give words to your bodily sensations (for example, clenching, pulsing, surging, heat, cold, numbness, vibrating).

- State the truth of your emotion as accurately as you can (for example, anger, frustration, sadness, fear, confusion, shock, dismay).

- Point out what you most need in one or two words (for example, validation, acceptance, understanding, patience, collaboration, safety, respect).

As you become more skilled with this, you can open it up to other people's perspectives (that is, actually listening to them, to truly understand them, versus waiting to make your point, vent your feelings, or insert blame). Your mindful honesty may allow them to speak their own truth. Maybe you'll end up with a truth-talking comrade!

Profile in Power: Emma Empowered

Prior to Valentine's Day 2018, Emma Gonzalez was just another senior at Marjory Stoneman Douglas High School in Parkland, Florida. After a shooter killed seventeen people that day, Emma and the other survivors of that attack on the edges of the Everglades became national and international figures at the center of the inflamed gun control debate.

A week after the shooting, more than a hundred Marjory Stoneman Douglas survivors channeled their anger over the lack of action in the wake of yet another in a long line of school shootings. They marched to the Capitol building in Tallahassee, Florida. Channeling the harnessed angry power of classmates like Emma, another student, Delaney Tarr, addressed legislators and said: "We want change ... We've had enough of thoughts and prayers. If you supported us, you would have made a change long ago ... We are coming after every single one of you, demanding that you take action!"

And then came Emma. "We call BS," she said, calling out politicians who support the National Rifle Association (the major public organization opposing gun control measures) and their lack of action. Her words went viral. Emma then helped organize the March for Our Lives rally on March 24, 2014—attended by well over a million people, the largest student protest in American history.

Speaking at the rally in Washington, DC, Emma turned her anger into poetic power. Not far from where Martin Luther King Jr. had stood on the Lincoln Memorial steps and described his dream, Emma faced the crowd with a poise and presence that transcended her mere eighteen years of age. After reminding us all that the shooter's spree in her school took place over six minutes, she led a six-minute moment of silence for the victims of the massacre. She channeled her indignation into one of the most compelling, powerful, and mindful moments in American social debate.

For Emma Gonzalez, anger's power echoed loudest in six minutes of penetrating silence.

If you're up for it, try taking six minutes of silence yourself right now. Listen into your mind and body as you do, and look at what power might be there behind your anger, and beneath other painful feelings and thoughts. Think and feel for the victims and their families of this and all school shootings. Think and feel for the survivors. Think and feel for our country. Think about and feel the power you might have within yourself.

Indignation as Ignition

All the listening you've been doing may have made it clear that there's something, or many things, in your life that are just plain wrong: people who are crossing your boundaries, or situations that are harming you and others. Maybe you're ready to stop ramming your head against things and, instead, foster a healthy state of indignation.

What if you could channel your anger at something unjust—something that is simply not right—into a strong displeasure that you could do something about? What if you could be someone who could help right such wrongs? Sound interesting? If so, mindfulness skills can help. Looking accurately at the situations and people sparking your anger is essential. To start, you need to build your patience muscle.

Developing mindfulness skills is how you build patience. In my own practice, personally and professionally, I've found that there are three components to building patience:

- Cultivating acceptance of what is actually here in the present moment

- Knowing that everything changes

- Not believing that you are separate from everyone and everything else

Patience may not be exciting, but it is crucial to well-being and effectiveness. And it's not something that only the Dalai Lama can do (with the proverbial "patience of a saint"). Patience is what modern psychological and brain science supports as creating more capacity for processing the huge demands on you in school, work, family, and friend situations; these demands can be really complex, and a lack of patience leads to more errors and missed opportunities for connection. Patience is also your greatest tool while you're waiting to make a difference via activism, advocacy, or standing up and being heard. Indignant patience is a slow-burning ember of sorts—it holds its heat and is portable. When your heat isn't setting everything on fire around you, you can move around and be flexible. You can wait for the right moment to use your heat to make change happen.

When we flare up with frustration or anger at others, or when we shut down and check out with loved ones, it's because we're losing touch with the three components of building patience. They are the essence of what mindfulness practice teaches. Out-of-control, angry impatience pulls the rug out from under our best intentions, especially with those who matter to us most. Being able to control the temperature of your anger is an advanced skill that's not that far off if you can really get these components deep into your bones.

Here are some suggestions for going beyond a passive view of patience, to making it the crucial skill it is—an important ingredient in making healthy indignation a force for good in your life.

Give It a Go: Wrangling Rage

Let's build your patience muscle as it relates to anger.

1. Sit in a comfortable upright posture as we've practiced in this book. With eyes closed, bring to mind a recent episode from your life in which you "unskillfully" managed your anger. Let yourself see the episode play out in your mind as though you're watching it on a movie screen.

2. Ask yourself, *Does my previous experience of anger toward another person or situation feel good? Does it make things more manageable, or less? Does it boost or block my mind? How might letting it fester negatively impact me and others? What are the costs of feeding my angry impatience?*

3. Ask yourself, *How might I learn something from the messed-up situations in my life? What might they have to teach me about my capacity for patience?* You don't have to like the pain they bring, but can you feel gratitude for this opportunity to expand your patience and capacity for motivated action?

4. As you end the meditation portion of this practice, silently make it your goal to ride out reactive urges or impulses. Make yourself accountable for

---

practicing patience. Commit to talking to others about what you've learned by listening to your past experience of anger and looking at the triggering sources of anger in your life. Feel the power of committing to making yourself accountable for surfing your anger with patience. Know that you will be on the lookout for opportunities for taking action that take everyone's needs into account.

5. And now, as you stand up and head into the rest of your day, stack the deck. Try to avoid situations where you're likely to lash out—when you're hungry or tired, for example. Rely on rituals and routines at times when you're likely to be fried and impatient. (For example, play video games to distract yourself from raging thoughts versus getting even more amped up by blasting people on social media.)

Some final thoughts about the role of patience in mastering your anger: Ask yourself whether you're surrounding yourself with people who feed your unhealthy anger, or those who support your healthy indignation when things are not right. One of the more challenging lessons in learning to harness anger is that some folks might be keeping us stuck based on how angry, negative, and toxic their influence on us is. And though these people may not be avoidable—a parent with a temper, for example, may be setting a bad example—it's still important and empowering to see what's happening, and how it affects you. You have the opportunity to choose a different life for yourself.

Give It a Go: Intention Conviction

In managing anger, it's crucial to look deep into the issue of intent—how people seem to be doing things *to* you (or you doing things *to* them, when you lash out) *on purpose*. So much of our unhealthy response to anger comes from overindulging false notions of people's intent.

Think of someone who ticked you off recently. Now ask yourself, *Did this person do this on purpose? If yes, were they intending to harm me? What conviction do they deserve?*

- First-degree douchebaggery (full and complete intention to harm; worthy of my rage)

- Second-degree douchebaggery (mostly on purpose, with some harmful intent)

- Involuntary douchebaggery (not really intentional; perhaps they lashed out without thinking or were already charged up about some other issue)

Now consider a time recently when you really ticked someone off. What degree of conviction do you deserve based on your intention alone?

- First-degree douchebaggery (full and complete intention to harm; worthy of others' rage)

- Second-degree douchebaggery (mostly on purpose, with some harmful intent)

- Involuntary douchebaggery (not really intentional; I lashed out without thinking or was already charged up about some other issue)

Last question: Do you think the person who recently got you so angry woke up that morning planning to stick it to you? Do you ever really arrange your whole day around making someone else's life miserable?

We tend to assume that others are scheming our demise, and thus, our anger and resentment are justified (as are our acts of vengeance and retribution). Yes, the person (and you when you've reacted with anger) may have been lashing out on purpose, but even in that moment, it was probably not really about you.

Angry action tends to be impulsive and centered on the moment at hand. We can get ourselves even more stuck in the trap of reactive anger when we assume that people are acting with premeditation—putting intent and planning behind their negative actions toward us. When we allow ourselves to look closely at what's really happening, intent usually loses some of its sting, and the conviction lessens to second degree or maybe even involuntary status.

If we see others' (and our own) anger with a clearer lens, what happens to the anger itself? We might just go from unhealthy, enraged friction to healthy, indignant ignition.

Because our brains are wired to snap to judgment and protect us from threats, we are all prone to a kind of tunnel vision—seeing less than the full picture of what's happening when we're all charged up with anger. Our anger actually keeps us from seeing clearly. Have you ever been flipping through channels on TV and come across one of those political talk shows? You know, where camera-hungry journalists and radical commentators are talking over each other, trying to prove themselves right and the other person wrong, often with raised voices and an occasional smirk or eye roll.

If you think about it, these segments are really silly. No one ever pauses after an opponent makes a point and says (without any sarcasm), "Hey, you know what? You're absolutely right! Thank you for helping me broaden my perspective and see things more accurately." If that actually happened (and the person saying it really meant it), CNN host Anderson Cooper would probably faint and fall out of his chair.

In learning to get on top of anger, it's helpful to start practicing what these political pundits seem incapable of—pausing and getting perspective on what's actually true in any anger-driven conversation (and inside us as well). This makes us stronger, not weaker.

With this activity, you're going to practice looking beyond the anger of the moment and seeing deeper possibilities for yourself.

Give It a Go: What Else?

On your TV or computer, go to one of the news channels (CNN, Fox, MSNBC—the more offensive, the better!). Sit comfortably and upright in a chair or on the floor (a straight back is best), and turn the volume all the way down. Now, do the following:

1. With your eyes closed, focus your attention on the flow of your breath in and out of your nostrils. Do so for a few minutes, focusing on the sensation of breathing, wherever you feel it most noticeably

(for example, tingling in your nostrils, rise and fall of your chest). Try to focus less on thinking about your breathing and more on noticing the sensations. If your mind wanders, that's fine—just gently come back to the sensation of your breath.

2. Now, for the next minute or so, shift your focus from your breath, and instead listen to any sounds you can notice in your immediate surroundings. Perhaps the ticking of a clock, air coming through vents, the hum of a refrigerator, city sounds outside. Pay attention to how the sounds come into your aware-ness and then pass away; let them come and go on their own.

3. Once you are feeling still and calm, turn up the volume on your TV or computer to a moderately loud setting—a bit louder than you would typically set it. Close your eyes again and continue notic-ing the sounds. Listen to the words and tone of the commentators. Focus on the sensations in your body that are prompted by the bickering, the arguing, and the drama from these arguments. If you find your thoughts getting caught up in the content of what they are debating, that's fine—just gently bring your attention back to the feelings in your body. Pay attention to any thoughts too as they arise, and just watch them, letting them come and go without grabbing onto them.

4. Continue listening and noticing for a few minutes. Let the reactions within your body and mind pass by without getting attached to or "hooked" by them.

5. Now, look past this situation and ask: *What else is happening here that matters to me? If I were looking down on this screen from the ceiling, what is just not right that needs to be fixed? If I were looking at it from space (assuming oxygen is available), what would make sense for actually solving these problems? What could I do with my frustrated energy? What might actually make a difference, if I could do or say it from a place of balance, of healthy indignation?*

What did you notice about your ability to give your attention to the anger and drama of others? What was difficult? What did you learn about your own habits? Did you want to argue back, or did you just want to get the hell away from it, or both?

When we're too caught up in shame and self-blame to let ourselves believe we could possibly fix things, it's a barrier to the healthy and motivating feeling of indignation. In the next section, we practice looking at this self-sabotage so that it's not blocking your ability to go from anger to action.

Messed-Up Messaging

Sam sat across from me during a therapy session and, after a long pause, looked up. "Did you know that the rings of Saturn are full of rocks and boulders?" he asked. Though his lack of participation in class and his apparent allergy to homework suggested otherwise, Sam was a storehouse of knowledge. Science in particular fascinated him.

"No, Sam," I said. "I didn't know that. Pretty cool that you do though."

Sam smirked away my compliment. It just didn't fit with how he'd learned to think of himself.

"It looks so beautiful and perfect from all these millions of miles away, but it actually is a worthless, orbiting heap of crap that gets reflected by the sun." Sam poked at a wad of Silly Putty I kept on my desk. He stabbed it, voodoo doll–style, with a pushpin from the bulletin board. The story he had told me about the cold-shoulder treatment he'd received from his mother that morning, his lesson about the worthless trash orbiting Saturn, and his Silly Putty abuse were obviously all connected.

Sam, and many kids like him, unfortunately learn from an early age that the adults in their lives think less than ideal things about them—sometimes directly telling them so. After enough repetition, they can begin to believe these messages. These messages become shameful scripts the kids continue to act out in their relationships with others, effectively blocking them from attaining the quality of connection and overall life satisfaction they deserve.

I told Sam he was a great debater, hardworking and kind, but when you've heard "stupid" and "ungrateful [insert your choice of demeaning expletive here]" hundreds, if not thousands, of times from your most important caregivers—the people charged with watering the seeds of your positive development—you're going to have trouble flowering.

Perhaps you've experienced messed-up messaging from adults. Perhaps because of these messages or your history of acting out in alignment with them (or both), you experience a high level of shame. If you do, you're probably finding it tough to get out of the trap that shame creates. It's like the thickest and deepest pit of quicksand—very tough to get out of it once you're in neck deep.

There's an important difference between guilt (or regret) and shame that is crucial in helping you harness your anger. Guilt, or regret, is a negative feeling about a specific action you've taken. It's helpful and appropriate for us to experience guilt when we've stepped over the line, when we've transgressed against others in our family, school, or communities. Regret is a universal emotion that prompts us to right wrongs and get ourselves back on track. We need guilt and regret in order to stay connected to others.

What we don't ever need is shame—a more pervasive self-punishment, an actual identity that solidifies around being "bad" in some way. There's self-inflicted pain involved with shame: *I'm wrong/bad/worthless/hopeless/unlovable/stupid.* Shame is a preoccupation with the past and a negative depiction of the future, in a way that blocks effective action and connection with others. If you're stuck in the quicksand of shame, you're not really listening closely to your thoughts and body, and you're definitely not looking carefully at what is truly present in the environment, in this moment.

Recent research suggests the heavy downside of shame. Science has shown a link between people's experience of shame and symptoms of serious depression—and a stronger link for shame than for guilt. Pervasive negative emotions like shame have also been associated with conditions such as coronary artery disease. Shame not only hurts us, it actually physically damages us.

Bottom line—you can't harness anger when you're chained to shame. You need to get rid of it. Because shame, unlike other painful feelings, is never a motivator. It only ever brings us down.

Selfie-Care: Self-Compassion

Taking selfies can be a way to connect with others, an expression of our fundamental need. But we sell ourselves short when we focus exclusively on what's on the surface. What if we learned to *really* take selfies? What if we used mindfulness to create self-compassion for ourselves?

If your anger has scorched your life sufficiently, you may have heard the knock-knock of shame popping up in your thoughts and emotions. That's actually a good thing! It's good intel to help you conquer one of the main obstacles to harnessing your anger.

Now you're ready for a heaping helping of self-compassion. According to psychologist and researcher Kristin Neff, self-compassion is self-kindness (versus self-judgment) combined with a sense of common humanity (versus being alone with what's hard) and mindfulness (versus being overidentified with bad feelings).

Self-compassion is the picture we should be taking of ourselves and posting for the world to see. It's us seeing our emotional pain as part of the larger, universal picture of being human, and seeing ourselves as worthy of kindness and care.

It's not weak or passive, not narcissistic or self-indulgent. It takes guts to do this work—and science shows that it can lower anxiety, stress reactions, depression, and perfectionism. And it can pull the rug out from under your old patterns of rage. It can open you up to your life, whereas your old patterns or reaction and judgment closed you down.

Some other reasons to practice self-compassion:

- It helps you feel strong and safe enough to lean in toward challenges and pain.

- There are numerous books and programs that can help you learn it.

- It connects you to yourself and others at the same time.

We spend far too much time in our heads—analyzing, judging, belittling, and criticizing ourselves. Self-compassion is the cure for that. Let's have a look.

Give It a Go: Self-Compassion Selfie

After an anger-related blowout, or after calling up some such episode from the past, take a moment to check in with yourself.

1. Direct your attention to your bodily sensations. Listen into where in your body you feel this upset. Feel these sensations just as they are for a few moments.

2. Now, step back into your mind and look at this emotional wreckage. Tell yourself something totally authentic that acknowledges this pain, like: *"This hurts"* or *"This sucks."*

3. Now, look again at the pain, and as you do, remind yourself that you're not alone. Say something reassuring to yourself that also ties you in to others who have dealt with this, like: *"Other kids have dealt with this too"* or *"All of us get stuck at some point."*

4. Give yourself a dose of self-care by saying something affirming that fits you and the situation—something like: *"I can choose to let myself off the hook,"* *"I can ride this anger out,"* *"I deserve to take care of myself,"* or *"I'm doing my best to turn my anger in a better direction."*

Do yourself (and the world) a favor by doing more than just reading this. Consider putting down your phone and taking a *real* selfie about how your anger is affecting things in your life and how you might feel better about it.

In the next exercise, we sidestep shame and get a more accurate picture as to how you might right your past wrongs.

Give It a Go: Picture the Possibilities

In a notebook or journal, draw a picture or write a scene depicting both the downside of your anger—the mayhem it has created for you and others—*and* the opportunities that exist for repairing and righting things.

Think of authentic apologies. Imagine doing the things that show your regret for having hurt others. Picture letting go of being right and instead doing the right thing—that will give you far more power than you might think. Combine the heaviness of the past and the lightness of the future into the same picture.

To keep yourself on the path to a healthier relationship with anger, it's important to protect yourself from the shame cycle, remind yourself of your successes, forgive yourself for your failures, and generally take good care of yourself.

Give It a Go: Self Interview

1. Imagine that you're being interviewed by a reporter (oh go ahead, imagine it's a cover story for *Rolling Stone*). The reporter asks for your "glory stories"—examples of things you've done and qualities you try to put into practice that you're proud of. Tune out your inner critic and give yourself credit for positive developments, milestones, and achievements large and small. Using your journal or notebook, what could you note in each of the following areas?

   - peers and friends

   - school

   - extracurricular activities

- hobbies and sports

- family

- leaps of faith and trust

- courage

- perseverance

- management of anger

2. Make an exercise plan if you don't have one already (better yet, get some others to do it with you) and commit to doing it! Write it down and keep track of what you do and don't do—taking notes helps make any habit much more likely to stick.

3. Commit to relaxing and soothing your mind and body. How might you do so without having a phone, remote control, or game controller in your hand? Try yoga, pick up a quiet hobby, meditate, listen to music, or simply hang out and talk with friends.

4. Drink water and eat something healthy on a daily basis. The fuse of anger is quicker to light when it's saturated with fats, carbs, and sugar.

5. Go to bed earlier than you think is morally permissible for someone your age. Just try it! At least once a week try going to bed far earlier than you would want your friends to know. Notice how you feel the next day. Make this a habit if at all possible, perhaps setting a reminder for once or twice a week. Your

inner crankosaurus is often brought out of hibernation by insufficient slumber.

Before moving on, pause again and look at the picture you drew in the activity earlier in this chapter. Try stepping away and looking at it again with a little more distance. What's it like to listen into the pain your anger has caused while looking toward possibilities for making things better? See how it's possible to simultaneously hold both your downsides (anger and shame) and upsides (repair possibilities). Mindfulness helps you hold much more than you may have thought possible.

Real Talk: Jump-Back Jack

Fourteen-year-old Jack had heard his parents and teachers telling him to "calm down" and "get ahold of your anger" for years. If it were as easy as flipping a switch, Jack would have turned off his rage long before he hit his teen years.

"I've tried everything to get my anger under control—even this meditation junk! Things might be better for a while, but my old habits always creep back in and get the better of me. It's really useless to keep trying! I'm sick of this crap and sick of people expecting me to just fix it!"

How might Jack put the listening, looking, and leaping skills from this book to work for him?

Mind-set Reset

Jack decided to start practicing mindfulness of his bodily sensations, and some relaxing breathing. His older brother was willing to practice along with him, and their parents promised to quit bringing up his anger issues in front of other family members and friends. Jack started noticing his negative self-talk (how much pressure he put on himself at school, being a "loser" with other kids, and how much of a "failure" he was for not beating his anger by now).

He started pausing, in the moment, to give himself a dose of self-compassion. As he learned to cut himself some slack, he noticed that his anger lost its power to shut him down. He found himself with more energy for stuff he really needed and wanted to get done.

"Healthy anger can be really motivating. Instead of just freaking out about a bad grade, now I turn around and study more. It's kind of like healthy stress—there's a way to channel it into something positive."

Jack is now jumping back. He no longer lets his old patterns of angry, frustrated thinking and feeling block his good intentions.

Nav Check

The point of this chapter is to help you realize that, with practice, you can begin to notice what's happening in your body and mind—without getting so hooked by the content of rigid, angry thoughts. It's like being a sportscaster, observing and talking about what's happening on the football field without actually being out on the field and getting bashed by a linebacker. Mindfulness gives us the space to look inside and outside ourselves and see the big picture—and thoughtfully choose what response is best—whereas mindless anger just creates more problems for us to fix. What's the big picture that's emerging for you? What's starting to matter to you that's perhaps becoming a bit more clear?

In the next chapter, we begin to learn how to harness what mindfulness has helped you learn about your anger. Instead of allowing your physical, mental, and emotional energy to gush out and muddy the ground you're standing on, you can choose to place your thumb over the edge of the open hose and aim your energy in directions that make sense, that put out "fires" and nourish the seeds of potential for what really matters in your life.

chapter 5

Using Anger as Fuel

About 58 percent of people experience anger that involves yelling or screaming a few times a week. About 10 percent report having episodes that involve physical aggression. Anger is a normal emotion, but how people manage it these days is problematic. Your education and upbringing probably haven't given you many tools for making it work to your (and others') benefit.

How many times have you said "Sorry" after your anger got the best of you? Do you carry with you that look on the faces of the people you've said it to? Anger is common and so is mismanaging it. People get numb to all the apologies when they don't seem to result in change.

Working your way through this book means that you're on a new track. You've been practicing listening into the anger in your thoughts and bodily sensations without getting stuck. You've also been learning to look more accurately at what's happening around you and getting a healthier, fuller perspective—and possible ways to make things better.

The trick is to break your old, autopilot reactive anger patterns and start doing things differently. Once you really start looking at the connections between yourself, others, and situations, you can start leaping toward actions that will show people that your "Sorry" actually means something.

You've gotten the message from your anger: Things are not right. Your needs aren't being met. Your sadness or worry have been neglected. Your desires have been ignored. People have hurt you. You've listened closely and gotten the message. Healthy indignation is growing in you.

Try the following activity to disable your autopilot.

Give It a Go: Lefty Loosey

Conjure up the name of someone you've been ticked off at. In your journal or on a separate piece of lined paper, write your name on the left side, and their name on the right, like this:

(Your name)	(Their name)

Now, write the names as quickly as you can on the next five lines, yours on the left and theirs on the right, like this:

(Your name)	(Their name)
(Your name)	(Their name)
(Your name)	(Their name)
(Your name)	(Their name)
(Your name)	(Their name)

Move your pen or pencil to your nondominant hand and write the same two names as quickly as you can on the next five lines.

Notice how much more your attention is required when you're not on autopilot. Anger reactions tend to be that way—they're easy in the sense that you can fly off the handle without being very aware of things. When you're listening and looking though, you're able to break the pattern and pay close attention to what's happening, and what seems to be driving the other person's behavior.

What happens if you get really curious about what's driving things for the other people involved? Especially if they're the ones making you angry.

Seeing with New Eyes

You may have heard the tale of Rip Van Winkle—the guy who walked off into the woods, got tired, took a nap, and woke up twenty years later to find that everything had changed. In this section (no, you don't get to take a nap), you'll practice looking at how things change, and actually seeing things in a new way with regard to how you manage anger.

We get so used to looking at things around us, that we usually see them the same way every time. When you look at your toothbrush in the morning, you probably don't think too much about it. But sometimes it's good to shake things up a bit.

Give It a Go: Rip Van Winking at Anger

In this activity, we're going to practice noticing what's "new" about stuff around you. When you practice looking for new ways to see something, you're less likely to look at it in old, maybe unhelpful (and stress-causing) ways.

1. Pick up an object you use every day. Maybe it's something in your room or backpack, or maybe it's your toothbrush—anything is fine. Sit comfortably, holding this object in the palm of your hand.

2. Breathe slowly and deeply and focus your attention on the object. Ask yourself, *What is this object for?* Notice what your mind comes up with—it's probably your usual way of thinking about it.

3. Now, breathe slowly and deeply again. Close your eyes and keep breathing until you notice yourself growing more calm and quiet.

4. Open your eyes and really look at the object. Explore with your senses—touch it, look it over carefully, tap it and listen to the sound, and smell or taste it (obviously, use your judgment!). Keep exploring until you notice something *new* about it.

5. Ask yourself, *Can this object be used for anything* other *than what I typically use it for?* Close your eyes and think about how you were able to learn new things, even about something you thought you knew everything about.

Take an object that reminds you of a situation in which you got really angry. Maybe it's a sheet of homework, a book from school, something you fought with your parents about, or a picture of someone on your phone.

Now, follow the same steps with *this* object. Stick with it until you notice that your angry thoughts and feelings about this object (and the person or situation it represents) change a bit. Keep looking and noticing new things.

Do you stay as angry when you look in new ways? If you're willing to get curious, does it change how you feel? If you had to make a decision and take some action about this person or situation right now, would you be more or less able to handle things effectively?

Next, give the following a try.

Give It a Go: Perspective Purifier

Let's take that special someone who's really gotten under your skin lately—parent, friend, teacher, or foe—and bring them vividly to your mind's eye. It's helpful if you can look for ways to drop the shame game, and the blame game.

To truly look is to see the full truth of things—you probably did not plan to be dealing with these challenges, and the world definitely didn't set out to block your every move. People are less focused on you than your mind wants you to think!

Put your imagined someone through the perspective filter below. Hold them in mind and ask these questions, noticing what happens as you do.

- You're Rip Van Winkle and you've just awakened from a twenty-year slumber in the woods. After picking off the bugs and cobwebs, consider the following: How old are you now? After that many years, what do you think about this other person you were so angry at so long ago? What do you make of the issue you were upset about? Does it still matter to you?

- You walk into a baby's nursery and see an adorable baby sleeping quietly in its crib. The baby's mother is standing there, looking down and smiling at her child as it sleeps peacefully. You stand next to her, also admiring the baby. You ask its name. The mother replies with the name of your foe—the one you're visualizing who's ticked you off. From this cribside point of view, what happens to your anger and resentment for this person?

- Imagine your foe sitting alone in their room, crying forcefully. What happens to your state of mind when you realize that this person is crying because someone very close to them has died—or the thing they care about most has been taken away forever? To witness that this person feels pain just like you and everyone else do—what does this do to your anger?

As we get ready for leaping, the third and final step in harnessing your anger, it's important to see the gift behind the anger people are giving you. They are (without intending to, I'm guessing) sending you important messages about the things that matter to you, things that are wrong and in need of fixing. Instead of making it personal—about the other person or about yourself—try to make it more about what you might change or fix, in yourself and in the world.

If you learn to look for these messages in your anger, you might not only disarm some of your excessive reactions to these folks but also get a shot of motivation to really say and do the things that will take your anger from the lowest depths of your day to the heights of what you're capable of. Get ready to go from anger to action!

Amor fati is a Latin phrase that translates to "love of one's fate." While it might seem a bit odd, it can be extremely helpful to learn to actually embrace our painful struggles. All the hardships, losses, and wrongs that led to your anger are facts of your history—there's no time machine for going back and changing what happened to what should have happened. Obsessing or wishing that what happened in the past hadn't happened, or had gone differently, only causes you more suffering.

For that matter, the same goes for resistance to what's happening right in this moment. If you can accept that things simply are what they are, without trying to change the things you cannot change, your life will be much happier and much more peaceful.

While you don't have to like pain or those who deliver it, you can learn to love what can grow out of your anger, and the other emotions that lie behind or beneath it. If you learn to work with them, these pains can become your possibilities—you might find yourself more compassionate, more focused, and more determined to make things better for yourself and others.

Give It a Go: Get Off Your "But"

This one is simple. Try going an entire day without making any excuses for any angry or impulsive reactions. Instead of replying to people with "but" and giving excuses or pointing out their own behavior and why they caused your angry reactions, simply take out the word "but."

Also, you might have ideas about productive things you could do with the energy of your anger—start an environmental clean-up drive, lobby friends to volunteer to be designated drivers, mentor younger kids who are struggling—*but* instead you end up telling yourself it's pointless and you won't make a difference.

Try using the word "and" instead. When you say "but" to someone or something, you're basically telling them that their (or your) feelings are inaccurate or outright invalid. When you use the word "and," you give others and yourself a slice of the truth.

It's hard to stay mad—and it's hard to stay passive—if you consistently get off your "but"s. If you stick with "and," it will keep reminding you that there's much more to the world than the narrow view of anger typically allows.

Profile in Power: Perspective Is Everything

In 1936, shortly before the outbreak of World War II, then twenty-two-year-old American rower Joe Rantz helped his team clinch Olympic gold in Berlin, Germany.

Joe had many reasons to be consumed by anger—his mom died when he was four, his stepmother neglected and abused him, and it was not long after that he had to find his own food after his family abandoned him altogether. When asked by his fiancée why his childhood did not leave him enraged, he said: "It takes energy to get angry. It eats you up inside. I can't waste my energy like that and expect to get ahead. When they left, it took everything I had in me just to survive. Now, I have to stay focused. I've just gotta take care of myself."

Balling up our fists and pounding on things in anger does not change the past, nor does it make our present or future any better. While anger is natural, getting stuck in it drains our energy away—energy that could better be used as fuel for doing what matters to us and might make a difference in our lives and in the world.

Your Inner Compass

In order to really get some good momentum going for yourself, it can help to spend a few moments getting clear as to what direction you're headed in. We all have an internal compass—an inner sense of what is right and wrong, and what we care about. These are the habits and tendencies that we don't have to be convinced of or rewarded for pursuing. We just do them because it feels right to do them.

My internal compass tells me that valued directions are creativity, connecting authentically with others, and having an impact on other people's lives. Notice that these are not simple goals—things that can be crossed off a to-do list or bucket list once they're accomplished. They really are more like basic directions that we can keep going toward indefinitely.

If you've been listening into your mind and body and hearing their messages, and if you're looking at yourself, others, and situations with more clarity, then you're likely moving toward a sense of what these directions might be for you. Out-of-control, misguided anger has a way of burning up your energy for more productive action. It's hard to get clear, for example, that you want to run a marathon when you're too angry to get your laces tied right!

Let's pause for a minute, to let you get as clear as possible regarding what actions you care about—what directions you want to go in.

Give It a Go: RESPECT

I'm betting there are at least one or two people you respect, people who truly treat you and others with the respect they deserve. Maybe your respectable person is a teacher, a coach, or an aunt or uncle. Maybe it's the mail carrier. Take a moment and walk yourself through the following questions:

- How exactly do the people you respect treat others?

- How do they communicate with you?

- How do these people manage, not just others, but themselves, when they're treated with disrespect?

- How might these people respect you?

- What have you done to earn their respect?

- What additional things might you do to earn even more respect from them (and others)?

Do the respect-worthy things this person does on a regular basis say anything about how you value these things? Look closely. And before you find yourself starting your next thought with the word "but," how about inserting the word "and" instead? They are worthy of respect for those actions *and* perhaps you might be as well.

Give It a Go: Commencement Speech

Let's take this internal compass thing even further. Imagine that you're sitting in your cap and gown and you're about to graduate (from high school, college, clown school—the educational setting doesn't matter). Imagine that you stand up, climb the stairs to the stage, and take your place behind the podium. You're giving the commencement speech. You're looking out at the sea of faces, many of whom are familiar to you, and you're telling them about the things you and others did that mattered to you—that got you to this place of transition into even bigger and better things for your life.

What things would you most want to be reporting about that you did on a regular basis—things worthy of respect and worth noting in a commencement speech? What were the wrongs you worked to make right?

Even if you're tempted to just roll your eyes and go about your day, I challenge you to give this a moment of honest, careful looking. See yourself up at the podium in your mind's eye (and ignore any heckling coming from your thoughts). What would you most want to announce about your actions in that speech? Might you consider commencing with these actions in your actual life?

Give It a Go: Mission Impossible Statement

Are you willing to make a wager with yourself? Consider making a prediction about the future you. What is your mission statement—your one-sentence declaration of independence from the ways in which anger has been holding you back?

Which causes and issues will you plant your flag in service of? Activism about disability or civil rights? Gun control? Speaking out against child or elder abuse? Entering the debate about climate change and protecting the environment? Maybe it's working to reduce the stigma about mental health issues, or helping at a suicide hotline. Homelessness?

Now, what are the changes you might make in your own life to repair the damage your anger has caused to others? What are the new habits you now want to pursue?

Your mission (should you choose to accept it) is to complete the following three-part statement with what fits for *you*:

- In beginning to listen to my mind and body, I've learned that anger is telling me that …. (Think of a specific

message your anger is relaying about what is important, wrong, or necessary for you; for example,
*I've been depressed and hiding my sad feelings and dark
thoughts behind the anger.*)

- With that message, I've begun to truly look at myself,
others, and situations more accurately and compas-
sionately and notice that .... (Think of a specific cause
or topic that you feel is a good direction for your
energy that used to be trapped by aimless anger; for
example, *I'm done with being a "helpless" victim of bullying
and want to help face down bullying for myself and others.*)

- This topic matters to me very much—so much so
that I'm willing to leap in that direction by .... (Think of
a specific habit or behavior you are committing to,
for example, *speaking up against cyberbullying.*)

If you're not able to fully complete this mission statement,
don't worry! It may seem impossible now, but it won't by the end
of this book.

Real Talk: From Bridge Burner to Bridge Builder

Jodie is a seventeen-year-old who developed a pattern of
pushing people away with angry nastiness, particularly at school
and with peers who had labeled her "loose" and "easy." The
shame she felt for some of the poor choices she'd made in an

attempt to feel liked and connected made her want to crawl out of her skin.

The shame and anxiety Jodie felt around others had been so severe when she was in middle school, that she learned that anger protected her. She was tall and strong and able to intimidate others. But while other kids (and some adults) were afraid of how big her anger could get, Jodie knew that people didn't really respect her. She had to add loneliness to the pile of bad feelings underneath her anger.

"Anger is a bitch. I like how it gets people to back up off of me and give me a little respect. I just wish it wasn't so intense sometimes. I wish I could work with it, kind of make 'friends' with it. The problem though is that anger doesn't play well with others. Then again—neither do I!"

Mind-set Reset

A friend (one of the few who stuck it out with Jodie) leaned in and spoke truthfully to Jodie about how "ridiculous" she had been behaving, and how their friendship would be over if things didn't change. "I think you're an awesome person on the inside," her friend said. "I and a bunch of others who care about you are just tired of the drama."

It was the wake-up call Jodie desperately needed. She started using a mindfulness app on her phone and realized how tense and tight her body was all the time. As she went deeper, she found feelings of sadness, anxiety, and shame that had been hiding out there. She had a heart-to-heart talk with her mom and ended up asking her school counselor if she'd be willing to be a point person for her to check in with at school when things felt stuck.

Jodie started exercising and remembered how much she had loved playing lacrosse when she was younger. She tried out for her school's team and became a leader on the squad during her senior year. Her size and strength now served a completely different, more productive, purpose. Now, she intimidated players on the field instead of peers in the hallway.

"I've learned that my anger is a sign that a deeper problem needs to be dealt with. I didn't realize that people weren't really respecting me—they were walking on eggshells so that I didn't give them crap. Anger and particularly getting aggressive is so off-putting, it's a very good deterrent. What I seemed to never get around to seeing until recently was how my anger was protecting the parts of me from feeling shame. And then, I'd feel ashamed for my awful handling of my anger. It was a vicious cycle, and I had to be the one to break it. I had to start putting the real deal of what was happening inside me out there, in order to get on top of it—to actually start getting real respect. Though I wish I didn't have to hurt so many people to get here, in a weird way I'm sort of glad I went through my 'anger years'—it made me who I am today and it helped me hang in with other people when they're struggling."

Nav Check

When you listen into your mind and body, you get accurate, detailed info about what's behind your anger. That puts things into perspective and gives you the clarity to see what matters most to you so that you can see the best direction in which to send your energy.

What have you noticed showing up for you in your mind and bodily sensations? Were you surprised by any of the "messages" that have popped up? Can you see how this increased detail and clarity might help you be more accurate as to the best, healthiest, most effective places to put the energy of your anger?

And now, with this third and final section of the book, we do the "leaping." Instead of your anger messing up everything you care about, now you can let all that anger actually go to work for you!

Part 3

Leap Toward Change

chapter 6

Action Is Power

Not only did famed Native American track-and-field athlete Jim Thorpe have to overcome the obstacle of racism to even make it to the 1913 Olympics in Stockholm, Sweden, he had to do it in scavenged, mismatched shoes! Someone stole Thorpe's shoes just before he was set to compete, and instead of losing his cool, he found two different shoes in a trash can, put extra socks on one foot to even them out since the shoes were different sizes, and then—no biggie—went on to win two gold medals!

Jim Thorpe was able to harness his frustration and not let it sideline him. That's what you will do as you move through this chapter. You've learned about mindfulness, and you've gotten perspective on what your anger is about and what matters to you. Now, I'm going to focus you in on action. We'll surge forward, to get your daily life moving in the direction you want it to—mismatched shoes, barefoot, however you show up.

New Tricks

You know the five-second rule for when you drop food on the floor? I recommend using the same rule for attempting any of the practice activities in this book—and even as you embark on any attempts to address the wrongs and injustices in your life, and the world. Here are the basic steps for putting this rule into effect:

1. Read the activity or consider the action you are about to take.

2. Listen into what shows up in your thoughts and bodily sensations. Listen closely for stinking thinking—reactive thoughts, rigid expectations.

3. Look at whether it matters to you that you give the activity a try.

4. Give yourself until the count of five to decide whether to take action. If it's a yes, try the activity with a solid, willing leap.

5. Listen to yourself again and notice what it was like to take mindful action regarding your anger. Notice the difference between what you usually do and how this felt and how things turned out.

We all have habits that are less than skillful, habits we developed as ways of coping with stress and emotional upset. Maybe for you it's how you quit things as soon as they start to get tough (or as soon as you anticipate failing). Or maybe it's about how you push people away with anger, or how gossipy texting and social media posting consumes your attention. These patterns all developed to try to get you respect, connection, something you wanted and didn't have.

That's why we need to build new habits: to help us break these less-than-helpful habits. The activities and strategies in this book can help you learn how to manage and channel your anger in more useful ways. Science suggests that if you hang in with a new behavior for at least twenty-one consecutive days, it becomes a habit that will stick with you. While building new habits around managing anger isn't easy, it's more doable than you think!

Give It a Go: Breaking Bad (Habits)

This activity is meant to help you rapidly apply the skills of listening from earlier in the book. It's what top athletes do before surging into the thick of things, and you too can use this to prepare yourself to take action on what your anger is calling for you to deal with.

1. Stand or sit upright and alert, with shoulders back and yet relaxed. Realize that your chest is open, that you're directly facing what is in front of you.

2. Take three deep, quick breaths into your belly, filling your belly with your breath and exhaling completely before the next breath.

3. Hold your breath for ten seconds, mindfully noticing what bodily sensations and thoughts pop up.

4. Take three slow, deep belly breaths, inhaling to at least the count of six, exhaling at least to the count of ten.

Do this before every activity you do in this book, and before any challenging action you're about to attempt, and watch how it helps you break up reactive or angry impulses. Watch how it gets you ready and steady for your most ferocious leaping.

Give It a Go: Authentic Apology

If you've lashed out at certain people in the past and caused them pain, you may be feeling some shame for having done so. As we talked about in chapter 4, things will only get worse if you stay stuck in the shame zone. Instead, let's use that healthy feeling of regret to fuel some positive action.

You've said "Sorry" many times in your life. Maybe you've even meant it, now and then. An authentic apology may not even have the word "sorry" embedded in it—but it often will have some kind of action in it. If you really regret what you did and the pain you caused someone, you may be able to take some kind of action, moving forward, to keep from causing that pain again—and you may want that person to know about it.

Here's how to use your healthy feelings of regret to repair a strained relationship with anyone in your life:

1. Ask the person for permission to say something important to them.

2. Make and maintain eye contact (not to turn this into a staring contest, but to let them see in your eyes that you're serious).

3. Tell the truth of what you did that caused them pain or upset. Say it in one sentence, and as a statement of the fact of what you did or said—*without any excuses attached.* That last part is important if you want to avoid causing more pain. (For example: "I was ticked off at you and went ahead and shared with our other friends what you texted me even though you said you wanted to keep it private.")

4. Acknowledge the damage done. Tell the person that you know this likely caused them pain, frustration, upset—again, with no excuses. (For example: "I would be really upset if someone did that to me. You have a right to be angry.")

5. Apologize and repair. Tell the person you're sorry (again, looking them in the eyes if possible) and how you're going to avoid making the same mistake in the future. (For example: "I'm so sorry I did that—that was wrong. From now on, I promise to honor your wish to keep what you say between us. I'll also try to tell you when I'm ticked so we can work it out, instead of just acting out.")

6. Let go of the urge to offer explanations and excuses, unless the person asks for them. With your new tools, you can act more carefully and thoughtfully in the future, and you should stay focused on this.

Under no circumstances should an apology from you include "I'm sorry you feel that way." Here's why—this is basically telling the person that, though you know they're upset, it's not your fault or your problem. You're making their pain invalid by implying that they've overreacted—it will only make things worse.

Remember the five-second rule with this activity. Listen to all the noise in your head and the jitters in your body, look carefully at why it matters to apologize, and—one, two, three, four—take the leap! It can feel scary to act with this kind of openness and vulnerability, but the truth is, it makes you stronger. It makes you the kind of person people want to be around, someone who has integrity and can be trusted.

Converting Anger to Action

Perhaps your journey into anger has sparked some fire in you. Instead of the out-of-control infernos that have raged in you in the past, perhaps you're ready to use this fire for good this time.

You can actually use your indignation: lean in, roll up your sleeves, and risk getting involved in helping make things better— at home, at school, and in your community. Use that fire in your belly to take a stand, use your voice, and put your energy into worthy causes.

Give It a Go: High Five

Use this activity to learn how to make your frustration work for you.

1. Place one index finger next to the bottom knuckle of the thumb on your other hand. Breathe slowly as you let your index finger climb up the outside of your thumb, pause briefly at the tip, and then descend the inside of your thumb as you slowly exhale. Continue breathing and moving your finger in this fashion, up and down each finger of that hand. Listen to your body and mind, and notice what's happening. Go *behind* the outer, self-protective armor of anger, and go *into* any other negative feelings that pop up.

2. Choose a cause or important issue that you care deeply about (for example, the environment, bullying, disability rights, drunk driving) and make it your "thing"—a primary way for you to channel your anger productively.

3. Slowly trace and breathe your way back across the fingers of your hand again (starting at the little finger this time and ending at the thumb), but this time, mentally assign each of your fingers an action for leaping into your selected cause. Link an action to each of your five fingers as you maintain smooth, even, mindful breathing.

4. Choose one of the fingers (actions) and keep it extended while folding the others down into the palm of your hand. This is your chosen action—the direction you will go in now.

5. Now do this thing, to support your cause. It can be as small as searching the Internet for how to volunteer in a local election campaign, or as big as—say your cause is bullying—texting an apology to someone you bullied in the past.

6. Put the five-second rule into effect. One ... two ... three ... four ... leap, my friend, leap!

Profile in Power: The Meter Maid

Hannah, a fifteen-year-old I once worked with, was furious about a number of things happening in her life at the time. She'd developed physically far faster than her female peers, and that led to lots of attention from boys, as well as envious nastiness from a number of girls.

After we did a lot of listening to and looking at her anger and the emotional pain beneath it, she came up with a personal power experiment for herself, and it definitely made a difference. Instead of fuming with frustration one weekend after being (yet again) left out of party plans, she made flyers on her computer at home and headed out the door on a mission.

The flyers contained the following, in a text box she pasted above a cool picture of a parking meter that happened to look like a face:

"Hello! I'm the Meter Maid, and I noticed your time was about to expire. I decided to insert some coins to prevent a ticket from sparking your ire! I now ask that you find a chance today to pay this act of kindness forward to another in a large or small way!"

Hannah then went to a nearby parking lot with meters and ticket-happy meter maids. She looked for expired meters and, after popping some quarters in, placed a flyer under the car's windshield wiper. Her anger at her situation had nothing to do with parking fines or meter maids, but this leap into random kindness to others made a difference for her that weekend. It may have for others as well.

Hannah then sat on a nearby bench and watched people come back to their car and discover the flyer. The smile on their face, the look they gave around the parking lot in search of their anonymous helper, and the fact that they kept the flyer as they got back in their car were evidence that she had converted the currency of her anger into something positive and valuable.

Most kids have experienced bullying in some fashion by the time they reach their teen years. The damaging effects of bullying are very clear (and with cyberbullying, the damage can literally go viral). If you've been a victim of bullying and harbor anger and resentment—or if you've bullied others in the past—this next activity may be a good leap for you.

Give It a Go: Flip the Bird

Have you heard of the Butterfly Project? It's for teens and adults who struggle with the impulse to self-harm (by cutting, for example) and asks them to be willing to ride out the impulse to cut, without following through. Here, we're going to apply a similar idea to bullying or cyberbullying.

1. When you're a bystander to bullying and feel like you don't want to speak up—or if you feel an urge to post something nasty about someone online, or outright bully them in person—take a pen and draw a small bird on your hand or arm. It's your bird of empowerment, rising up like the mythical phoenix from the ashes of anger.

2. Name the bird after a victim of bullying if you want, or decorate it—but don't scrub it off. Next time you end up failing to speak out about bullying you witness, or if you lose control and end up bullying someone yourself before the bird flies away (fades out) on its own—*it dies*. If you take action on behalf of a target of bullying or if you avoid an impulse to bully, it lives on even after it fades away.

3. Another person may draw birds on you, particularly if you've shared with them about how you're working to help bring awareness to bullying. These

birds deserve extra care and attention. It's awareness about bullying that keeps it out of schools and communities.

4. Consider taking another leap: either righting a wrong caused by your past unskillful response to bullying, or building something new that makes things better. Think authentic, reparative apologies. For example, you can let your bird fly by talking to a younger sibling or cousin about how you're working to get a better handle on your anger.

Exactly what you do isn't as important as the fact of your doing it—your intention to either repair or build something new that will help make bullying less a part of you and your friends' reality.

Let's shift gears to another important topic for modern teens. Are you frustrated with what adults in government have been saying and doing—or not saying or doing—with regard to protecting the environment? Here's an activity that gives you a chance to take the energy of indignation and spray that hose on some flowers!

Give It a Go: Compost It

Organic gardeners know that the best flowers require compost in order to grow well. Let's take the manure from your past or present experience of anger and compost it into a healthier future.

1. Pause right now and listen into your body and mind. If there's rigidity, blame and shame, or physical sensations of rage, sadness, depression, or anxiety—whatever heaviness is there, don't worry, it's nothing more than manure. We can use it all.

2. Let the difficult feelings in your mind and body just be inside you as mere energy, like water backed up behind a huge dam that's ready to crack.

3. Now go to a window or walk outside and look at something in the natural world, something you might be able to use this energy inside you to make better. Feel the energy of your anger or heaviness— even if it came to you from a dark source (like abuse, trauma, or extreme hardship)—and imagine how you might turn the garbage from your life history into something beautiful. What is something—small, medium, or large—that you could take a stand on, that you could use the raw material of your pain to build up?

4. Listen ... look ... and now (five-second rule) ... leap! Put into action a plan to convert your anger currency, to make flowers from garbage.

   • Resentful that others have carved up the natural beauty of your neighborhood? How about writing a story or play about the damage done?

- Angry at mindless people trampling on the environment to the detriment of us all? Convert your anger into a rap or song that connects this with your not being heard, or your feelings being trampled on, in some area of your life.

- Anger left you feeling defeated at school? How about picking up a new outdoor hobby (like kayaking or hiking) that gets you outside and moving toward a feeling of victory?

- Has rage razed your relationships to the ground? How about clearing a patch somewhere—in a community garden, perhaps, or even just in a pot on your window sill—and growing something?

- Heart clogged by sadness and loss? Go outside and pick up litter before it clogs up our world.

- Insulted by important people in your life? Mentor someone younger, and do something together to take better care of nature than the two of you have been treated by others.

Give It a Go: The M&M Game

The heat of your anger will melt everything in your life if you let it. What if you turned up the heat in a more controlled, mindful way? Let's play the M&M game.

1. Get some M&Ms and put them in a bowl. Find a few friends to play too.

2. Sort the M&Ms by color. Assign each color an action. For example:

- Brown—Connects you with your closest friends

- Red—Excites you and makes you want to show up

- Green—Makes you feel powerful and effective

- Blue—Gives you a sense of accomplishment

- Orange—Gives you courage to take responsibility

- Yellow—Makes you feel grateful to someone who had your back

3. Everyone claims a color (or two) and takes turns offering an M&M to another player. In order to eat the M&M, the receiving friend must say what activity gives them the associated result. If they don't, or can't, they have to collect one M&M from every other player.

4. The first player to have given away (or eaten) all the M&Ms in their possession wins.

The point of this game is to get you and your friends talking and thinking about things that matter to you.

The Five Ws

Another factor that really helps in mindfully harnessing anger is building an understanding of what is good timing for taking action. Think about the last time you were truly angry.

Ask yourself the following W questions, as they relate to that situation. They will help you see behind and beyond the limits of impulsive, reactive, directionless anger. For any specific anger episode, ask yourself:

- **Who** is affected by my anger, both directly and indirectly, and am I considering their needs?

- **What** deeper messages of my anger do I need to address?

- **When** is it wise for me to pay attention to my mental and physical experience of anger, and when is it wise, instead, to temporarily distract myself or focus on calming things down?

- **Where** am I right now, and how might this environment be intensifying my anger?

- **Why** do I deserve credit for working to manage myself more skillfully?

Real Talk: All Dolled Up

Laurie, eighteen years old, was quick to lash out at others. No one—including her parents—seemed to realize she was depressed and suicidal. She'd even written suicide notes that she'd left out in her messy room, but no one noticed.

"Not too long ago, my little sister came into my room and started touching stuff when I wasn't around. She's always getting into my stuff and telling our parents about what she finds, and I get blasted as a result. I think she enjoys screwing up my life. So what did I do? I pushed past her and went into her room and trashed her precious doll collection. Tossed a few of the little angel's favorites out her window and onto the lawn. If my parents keep believing she's perfect and aren't going to ever do anything about her, then I'll have to take care of it myself."

Can you listen to this young woman's angry thoughts and hear below them to the pain underneath? Can you feel how narrow her perspective has become as a result of letting these thoughts fester and grow?

Can you imagine what it must be like for Laurie to lie on her bed and see a suicide note she'd written months before sitting untouched on the floor of her room? What it must have felt like in her body and sounded like in her thoughts to realize that no one knew how much sadness and hopelessness were building inside her?

Mind-set Reset

Thankfully, Laurie's math teacher—Ms. Sawyer, whom Laurie had always liked—saw past her crusty, angry surface. After class one day, she gently suggested that she thought it would be good for Laurie to talk to someone. Laurie refused to talk to her guidance counselor, but she was willing to see a therapist outside of school.

Ms. Sawyer helped Laurie write a text to her mom asking to see the therapist, and since Ms. Sawyer had been so kind and helpful, Laurie followed through and went to the appointment her mom set up for her.

In therapy, Laurie learned to notice and listen to the discomfort of the sadness inside her when it began to show itself like a scared, timid animal. The therapist helped Laurie look past her blaming and hopeless thinking to see how the anger was protecting her from the pain of the sadness. Now that Laurie could see and feel the sadness, the anger wasn't needed as much. The sadness could now show itself and get taken care of.

"Anger is a red flag that something inside you is wrong—out of whack. It helps me know that there's something I care about or need that is trying to get my attention. Anger isn't bad by itself. It's biological, and when I'm responsible with it, everyone can benefit."

Now she's got some momentum. Not only is this teen listening to what her anger is trying to say, she's also looking toward how it can serve as a spark—a touchpoint—for making positive changes. She's seeing things so much more clearly and now has the potential to make things better at home with her sister and parents, and with others as well. She's now doing some serious leaping, with mindful action, learning from and using the energy and intelligence of her anger.

Laurie is currently away at college and volunteers for an advocacy group as a Mental Health Awareness Ambassador. She recently returned to her high school and gave a talk to new freshmen about the importance of reaching out, finding support, and not using anger to fix your problems.

Nav Check

You've made it to the end, and for that you deserve high praise. Well done, you!

We've navigated through the steps of mindful management of your anger, and you've hopefully learned a bit about yourself, your anger, and how you might use it as fuel in the future. Are you willing to keep going with all the skills you've picked up in this book? Are you up for a habit of harnessing anger for powerful action from this point forward?

Pause here, for just a moment, to really feel all you've learned. Working to create a new relationship to your anger is not a one-and-done situation—it takes time, practice, and ongoing commitment. Here's to having the strength and intelligence required to do the work—and to hopefully leaving the worst of your anger behind you!

Break the Dam—
Let Your River Flow

My grandmother used to cheat when we played card games like Baseball in the soothing shadows of her living room. She would massage the rules and let me win all the spare change from her purse. I loved these games with her, sitting and listening to the warm silence of her house, broken only by the ticking of her old clock.

Here's something else I remember—my grandmother driving her van, using a mocking sing-song voice and complaining about anyone in the family who had committed an unforgivable offense that week. "If she thinks I'm going to talk to her again, then she has another thing coming." As a kid, I wondered what "another think" was, but from the anger in her voice, maybe I was better off not knowing.

As is the case with all of us, my grandmother had light and dark aspects. She wasn't perfect. Many of us yell, blame, get defensive, lash out, and shut down because we want to feel better—we want to be happy and free of pain. We don't realize that our behavior is only making things worse and making our pain greater.

My grandmother, again like all of us, frequently played an angry tug-of-war with the people in her life who sparked upset in her. Unfortunately, her oldest son—my uncle—was often the target of her resentment. Stretching back to his own teen years, and even earlier, his conflict with my grandmother grew to a level of toxicity between them that poisoned their later years. Unfortunately, before my grandmother passed away, my uncle didn't learn about listening, looking, and leaping past his anger and resentment. He never had the chance—he never took the chance—to make things better with her, and then it was too late.

The research is clear. Holding on to anger and resentment not only feels unpleasant (and makes you unpleasant to be around), it can also be damaging to your health. Study after study have shown the destructive effects of long-held, intense anger. When we hold on so tight in these angry tugs-of-war and pull so hard for years, decades, is it any wonder that the body gives out? And not just the body; the mind—our capacity to learn, understand, and connect with the world—also suffers from the struggle.

There are no quick fixes when it comes to changing ingrained patterns of anger. If we try to change too drastically or suddenly—if we move too far, too fast from our baseline level of functioning—it can be too hard for the system to adapt, and the changes are usually very tough to maintain. Old habits return if we haven't first built up support for our new habits.

A smoker who quits cold turkey has to publicly commit to the change—has to avoid old smoking buddies. Someone who quits drinking might need to forgo bars and clubs for a while. And teens trying to walk away from their destructive, angry ways may need to avoid engaging with the people who most trigger their anger—possibly because those people have anger issues of their own.

It's hard, this work, but it will change the course of your entire life. Don't give up! Hang in there. Listen deeply to your body and mind when you're angry, look for the sources of motivation for change inside yourself, and soon you'll be leaping into the happy, healthy future you've created for yourself.

My greatest hope is that you are able to use the tools you've found here to dig your way out of shame and blame, so that the cycles of anger and resentment don't dam up your life. You deserve more. Put your anger to work for you, rather than letting it take over your life.

Imagine the direction you want to go in, where you want your future to lead you. Set your navigation coordinates. And then go for it. You can do it. You can go wherever you want to go if you're willing to work hard to get there. You may just find, along the way, that working hard for something important feels good. It makes you someone who other people want to be around, want to have on their team.

Martin Luther King Jr. said this of anger: "If I wish to compose or write or pray or preach well, I must be angry. Then all the blood in my veins is stirred, and my understanding is sharpened."

May your blood be stirred and your understanding sharpened. May you find peace on the journey from anger to action!

Acknowledgments

This book is dedicated to my daughter, Celia. Though you're not yet a teen, you have taught me so much about what it means to "lean in" with tough feelings and situations. Your courage and perseverance are such an inspiration to me, and to many people in your life.

This book has also been made possible with the "hurdle help" of my wife, Lisa; my son, Theo; and the hundreds of young students and clients who have helped me learn to see behind behavior the prizeworthy truths that are always there inside of others—even angry folks! A deep bow of gratitude to the folks at New Harbinger (Jess O'Brien and Caleb Beckwith in particular) as well as the crucial and creative help of developmental editor Teja Watson, and the attention-to-detail "laser" of copyeditor Karen Schader. This book will resonate with teens in large part because of her thoughtful help with the manuscript.

My greatest hope is that this book truly helps teens harness their power. Every teen deserves a chance to rise up, be heard, and be helped to make a meaningful difference with their lives.

Resources

Mobile Apps

Headspace: https://www.headspace.com

Insight Timer (meditation timer): https://insighttimer.com

Stop, Breathe and Think: https://www.stopbreathethink.com

Card Decks of Coping Skills Practices

Growing Mindful: A Deck of Mindfulness Practices for All Ages. PESI Publishing and Media.

Growing Happy Card Deck: Positive Psychology Practices for Teens and Adults. PESI Publishing and Media.

Websites

Inward Bound Mindfulness Education (iBme)
This nonprofit offers in-depth mindfulness programming for youth and the parents and professionals who support them. Their programming guides teens and young adults in developing

self-awareness, compassion, and ethical decision making, and empowers them to apply these skills to improving their lives and communities.

https://ibme.info/about/

Teen Line
This nonprofit organization helps teens get connected to support and resources for addressing their problems. It provides personal teen-to-teen education and support in order to help prevent problems from becoming a crisis, using a national hotline, current technologies, and community outreach.

https://teenlineonline.org

Mitch R. Abblett, PhD, is a clinical psychologist and former executive director of The Institute for Meditation and Psychotherapy, a nonprofit focusing on education and training at the intersection of mindfulness and treatment. For over a decade, he was clinical director of Manville School, a Harvard-affiliated therapeutic day school program in Boston, MA, serving children with emotional, behavioral, and learning difficulties. He maintains a private psychotherapy and consulting practice, and writes about mindfulness, professional development, and family mental health for *Mindful* magazine (Mindful.org). His books include *The Heat of the Moment in Treatment* for clinicians, *The Challenging Child Toolbox*, and *The Five Hurdles to Happiness*. He also coauthored *Mindfulness for Teen Depression* and the child/family-friendly practice aid *Growing Mindful*, as well as additional mindfulness-related card decks. He conducts national and international trainings regarding mindfulness and its applications. Learn more at www.drmitchabblett.com.

Foreword writer **Christopher Willard, PsyD**, is a psychologist and educational consultant based in Boston, MA, specializing in mindfulness. He currently serves on the board of directors at the Institute for Meditation and Psychotherapy, and is president of the Mindfulness in Education Network. He is author of *Child's Mind*, *Growing Up Mindful*, *Raising Resilience*, and three other books. He teaches at Harvard Medical School.

More  Instant Help Books for Teens

An Imprint of New Harbinger Publications

**THE ANGER
WORKBOOK FOR TEENS,
SECOND EDITION**

Activities to Help You Deal
with Anger & Frustration

ISBN: 978-1684032457 / US $17.95

STUFF THAT SUCKS

A Teen's Guide to Accepting
What You Can't Change &
Committing to What You Can

ISBN: 978-1626258655 / US $12.95

**THE RESILIENCE
WORKBOOK FOR TEENS**

Activities to Help You Gain
Confidence, Manage Stress &
Cultivate a Growth Mindset

ISBN: 978-1684032921 / US $16.95

**CONQUER NEGATIVE
THINKING FOR TEENS**

A Workbook to Break the Nine
Thought Habits That Are
Holding You Back

ISBN: 978-1626258891 / US $16.95

**DON'T LET YOUR
EMOTIONS RUN YOUR
LIFE FOR TEENS**

Dialectical Behavior Therapy Skills
for Helping You Manage Mood
Swings, Control Angry Outbursts
& Get Along with Others

ISBN: 978-1572248830 / US $17.95

**MINDFULNESS FOR
TEEN DEPRESSION**

A Workbook for
Improving Your Mood

ISBN: 978-1626253827 / US $16.95

new harbinger publications
1-800-748-6273 / newharbinger.com

(VISA, MC, AMEX / prices subject to change without notice)

Follow Us

Don't miss out on new books in the subjects that interest you.
Sign up for our Book Alerts at **newharbinger.com/bookalerts**